WENDY COPE

Rory Waterman

NORTHCOTE

WENDY COPE

Writers and Their Work, launched in 1994 in association with the British Council, won immediate acclaim for its publication of brief but rigorous critical examinations of the works of distinguished writers and schools of writing. The series embraces the best of modern literary theory and criticism, and features studies of many popular contemporary writers, as well as the canonical figures of literature and important literary genres.

First published in 2021 by
Liverpool University Press
4 Cambridge Street
Liverpool L69 7ZU

This paperback edition published 2023

on behalf of
Northcote House Publishers Ltd
Mary Tavy
Devon PL19 9PY

British Library Cataloguing-in-Publication Data
A catalogue record for this book is available from the British Library

ISBN 978-1-80085-952-4 cased
ISBN 978-1-80207-787-2 paperback

Typeset by Carnegie Book Production, Lancaster
Printed and bound by CPI Group (UK) Ltd, Croydon CR0 4YY

Contents

Acknowledgements

In December 2018, I emailed Wendy Cope. I had then never met or corresponded with her, and wanted to let her know I intended to write this book – would she mind answering my questions and sharing any unpublished material not available in her archive? In my experience, some poets prefer not to come under critical scrutiny, and I was not sure I would receive the response I was hoping for. Since that time, she has been nothing but a wonderful support, inviting me into her home to pore through her recent drafts and ephemera, answering my many questions about points of fact, and otherwise not attempting to influence anything I write – which is of course essential. She has made the writing of this book even more pleasurable than I had expected, and has thus far read none of it: I was keen to maintain critical distance, and she made it easy for me to do so. I am also very glad to have spent some time with her husband, the poet and critic Lachlan Mackinnon. He has maintained equal distance from what I have written, and is one of a handful of poetry critics who sets the bar very high for the rest of us.

I am also grateful to Faber & Faber for granting permissions, the staff at the British Library (especially Callum McKean) for helping me to navigate the library's Wendy Cope archive before it had finished being catalogued, the journal *English* for publishing an article that drew on my research ('"The Nation Rejoices or Mourns": Literary and Cultural Ambivalences in Wendy Cope's *Making Cocoa for Kingsley Amis*'), the Faculty of Arts and Humanities at Nottingham Trent University for funding a research trip and granting a semester's research leave, and Alan Jenkins *of The Times Literary Supplement* (*TLS*) for commissioning a review of *Anecdotal Evidence* in 2018, which encouraged me to conceive of this book. I am also very grateful to

Liverpool University Press and Northcote House, and especially Christabel Scaife and Brian Hulme, for taking on the book, and to Christabel and her colleagues for supporting it through to completion.

Biographical Outline

1945	Born in Erith, Kent, to Fred Stanley Cope, chairman and managing director of a department store, and Alice Mary Hand, his secretary before they married, and then a director and company secretary.
1949–50	Attended West Lodge Preparatory School, Sidcup, Kent.
1950–3	Attended Convent of the Sacred Heart, Erith.
1953–7	Attended Ashford School for Girls, Ashford, Kent.
1957–62	Attended Farringtons School, Chislehurst, Kent.
1963–6	Attended St Hilda's College, Oxford, to study history.
1966–7	Attended Westminster College, Oxford, to study for a Diploma of Education.
1967–9	Primary school teacher in Newham, London.
1969–81	Primary school teacher, and eventually deputy headteacher, in Southwark, London.
1980	Publication of first poetry pamphlet, *Across the City*. Four more pamphlets would follow in the 1980s.
1981–4	Seconded to County Hall to work on Inner London Education Authority newspaper.
1982	Publication of *Poetry Introduction 5*, containing a selection of Cope's poems. Her first publication with Faber.
1984–6	Part-time primary school teacher in Lewisham, London.
1986	Publication of *Making Cocoa for Kingsley Amis*.
1986	Stopped teaching and became a freelance writer.
1987	Awarded Cholmondeley Award.
1988	Publication of *Twiddling Your Thumbs: Hand Rhymes*.
1989	Publication of Cope's first anthology, *Is That the New Moon? Poems by Women Poets*.

1991	Publication of *The River Girl.*
1992	Publication of *Serious Concerns.*
1993	Publication of Cope's anthology *The Orchard Book of Funny Poems.*
1994	Moved to Winchester to live with new partner, the poet Lachlan Mackinnon, who taught at Winchester College.
1995	Awarded American Academy of Arts and Letters Michael Braude Award for Light Verse.
1998	Voted listeners' choice in BBC Radio 4 poll to succeed Ted Hughes as Poet Laureate. Makes it clear publicly that she wouldn't want the role.
1998	Publication of Cope's anthology *The Funny Side: 101 Humorous Poems.*
2000	Publication of Cope's anthology *The Faber Book of Bedtime Stories.*
2001	Publication of *If I Don't Know.*
2001	Publication of Cope's anthology *Heaven on Earth: 101 Happy Poems.*
2002	Publication of *George Herbert: Verse and Prose,* edited and introduced by Cope.
2007	Judged the Man Booker Prize.
2008	Publication of *Two Cures for Love: Selected Poems 1979–2006.*
2010	Appointed Officer of the Order of the British Empire (OBE).
2010	Publication of *Going for a Drive.*
2011	Wendy Cope archive acquired by the British Library.
2011	Publication of *Family Values.*
2011	Moved to Ely, Cambridgeshire.
2013	Married Lachlan Mackinnon.
2013	Publication of *Time for School.*
2015	Publication of *Life, Love and The Archers.*
2017	Publication of *Christmas Poems.*
2018	Publication of *Anecdotal Evidence.*
2018	Publication of *Saint Hilda of Whitby.*
2019	*Serious Concerns* republished as part of a series of ten collections, to celebrate ninety years of Faber.

Abbreviations

AE	Wendy Cope, *Anecdotal Evidence* (London: Faber, 2018)
DSL	Wendy Cope, *Does She Like Word-Games?* (London: Anvil Press, 1988)
FV	Wendy Cope, *Family Values* (London: Faber, 2011)
GFD	Wendy Cope, *Going for a Drive* (London: Collins, 2010)
IIDK	Wendy Cope, *If I Don't Know* (London: Faber, 2001)
LLA	Wendy Cope, *Life, Love and The Archers* (London: Two Roads, 2014)
MBA	Wendy Cope, *Men and Their Boring Arguments* (London: Wykeham, 1988)
MC	Wendy Cope, *Making Cocoa for Kingsley Amis* (London: Faber, 1986)
PI	Wendy Cope, *Poetry Introduction 5* (London: Faber, 1982)
RG	Wendy Cope, *The River Girl* (London: Faber, 1991)
SC	Wendy Cope, *Serious Concerns* (London: Faber, 1992)
TCL	Wendy Cope, *Two Cures for Love: Selected Poems 1979–2006* (London: Faber, 2008)
TFS	Wendy Cope, *Time for School* (London: Collins, 2013)
TYT	Wendy Cope, *Twiddling Your Thumbs: Hand Rhymes* (London: Faber, 1988)

Introduction

Wendy Cope's first two collections, *Making Cocoa for Kingsley Amis* and *Serious Concerns,* have together sold almost half a million copies; most poets' collections sell in the hundreds. In 1998, when Ted Hughes died, she was the BBC listeners' choice to succeed him as Poet Laureate – a position she has consistently made clear she would not want – and in 2010 she was awarded an OBE for services to poetry.[1] Moreover, her work has been admired by a disparate array of poets. Hughes congratulated her 'deadpan fearless sort of way of whacking the nail on the head' (*TCL* back cover).[2] Peter Reading wrote to Cope admiringly about her first book.[3] Carol Rumens referred to her second as 'a classic'.[4] Gerry Cambridge commended Cope for fulfilling Robert Frost's 'definition of poetry' – that it 'should be "common in experience, uncommon in writing"'.[5] And the former Archbishop of Canterbury Rowan Williams – who is also, if less famously, a poet – has said that she 'is without doubt the wittiest of contemporary English poets, and says a lot of extremely serious things'.[6] She has also been celebrated as one of the finest parodists of her, or any, generation. In *The Oxford Book of Parodies,* for example, Cope is represented by the third highest number of contributions (seven), beaten only by Max Beerbohm and Craig Brown (both with eight).[7] It is perhaps surprising, then, that her popular appeal has been met with critical near-silence. After five major collections and more than a third of a century into an extremely successful poetic career, Cope has received only piecemeal critical attention, mostly confined to book reviews. This is the first monograph on her work.

Why should this be so? Her predominant style likely has much to do with it. As A. M. Juster notes, Cope has written 'primarily formal poetry at the highpoint of its disfavour within the academy'.[8] Her penchant for rhyme and metre – the caveat being that some of her most celebrated poems use neither – is shared with many of the post-war British poets most popular with a wider reading public, such as John Betjeman, Charles Causley, and Philip Larkin; in academic circles, however, the only one of these poets to receive much attention is Larkin. Moreover, critics have 'rarely credited Cope for anything other than simply being funny; they passed over her range of styles and subjects, her ideas, her concision, her erudition, her unpredictability, and her mastery of form' (Juster). Julie Kane, who praises Cope's 'irreverent content' and her habit of 'recycling forms from the past with no particular allegiance to them', agrees with Juster, writing that 'many academics seem to have mistaken Cope's stylistic timeliness for its opposite, anachronism'.[9] Ian Gregson, who mourned Cope's 'immense popularity', provides a particularly hostile example, ignoring what she does do and focusing instead on what she does not, to characterise her as 'crudely anti-modernist'.[10] Even some of her kinder critics have a history of qualifying their praise rather emphatically. Reviewing Cope's *Selected Poems* in 2008, Henry King described her ambivalently as 'a world champion lightweight poet';[11] and in 2014, Rebecca Watts admired the 'insight and poignancy' of some of Cope's poems, but wondered 'how much actual pen-time' they had required.[12] In 1986, Richard O'Brien summed up the broader critical consensus, which has lazily endured, by claiming that her wit is 'her strength and her limitation'.[13]

Michael Schmidt was alert to that when, in 1998, he noted:

> Dismissed as a writer of 'light verse', she has been critically undervalued. The poems are funny at times, skilful always, and formally resourceful. If we regard Skelton and Gascoigne as 'light', then she is 'light', but in the sense of illumination rather than of weight.[14]

Others have also praised her work, albeit in passing, by counteracting the implicit dismissal of her as a light-versifier: the famously excoriating critic William Logan has admired her for her 'cunning' and for 'expos[ing] the whole banquet of male sensibility',[15] Nicola Thompson has written enthusiastically about her 'genius' and 'subver[sion]',[16] and Anthony Thwaite has called her poems 'brilliantly observed and cunningly written', and noted that she is 'a subversive and sly commentator on sex'.[17] It is worth highlighting these repeated notions that Cope's poetry is cunning and subversive – and it is clear that, for these critics, deeper engagement with Cope's work does not lead to the conclusion that it is all lightweight. However, none of them have written about her poetry at length. The present volume addresses this gap in literary criticism, and comprises a timely study of one of our most critically neglected major poets.

The aim of this book is to provide incisive critical comment on Wendy Cope's poetry and how this has developed, and to assert her place in the canon of modern British poetry. It takes a largely chronological approach, guiding readers through shifts in Cope's poetic aesthetic over time. Her volumes of children's poetry are then considered in a separate chapter – with references back, where necessary, to her main collections. The final chapter considers the 'uncollected Cope': poems included in pamphlets but left out of books, unpublished poems, and poems completed since *Anecdotal Evidence* (2018), and hence not yet considered for a collection. In many cases, the work she did not choose to publish or collect sheds light on the directions in which Cope was taking her more familiar poetry. I have largely avoided referring to her uncollected poems in the preceding chapters, as to do so would have been to dilute the focus on each collection as a discrete work. The chosen methodology points readers towards those connections without distracting from the consideration of each volume as it stands, and the book ends with comment about where her work is now heading. The chapters are, as much as possible, self-contained, so that they might be useful to readers if read individually. However, across the whole book a narrative emerges, of the development of a poet both marginal and major.

1

'I learned to get my own back': *Making Cocoa for Kingsley Amis* (1986)

Wendy Cope gained a huge reputation in the early 1980s mainly for a series of witty and incisive parodies, often under the name of her desperate fictional *poète maudit* Jake Strugnell: as Anthony Thwaite puts it, she found 'her own voice [...] as a parodist'.[1] This was part of her apprenticeship as a poet: as she has noted, 'To write a good parody of somebody's work you really have to look at it very carefully, so you learn a lot.'[2] Many of these first appeared in major press outlets such as *The Spectator* and *The Observer*, as well as on the BBC and in popular magazines such as *Vogue*, and were eventually collected with many other poems, some of which were more ostensibly personal, in her debut collection, *Making Cocoa for Kingsley Amis*. When that book appeared in 1986, prompting one Canadian newspaper reviewer to claim hers was 'the first collection of verse in a long time that has made me laugh aloud',[3] it made bestseller lists, selling in quantities almost unheard of for a poetry collection.[4]

Making Cocoa for Kingsley Amis also inspired vitriol, directed towards both her and her audience. Reviewing it in *PN Review*, one of Britain's most prestigious poetry magazines, Peter Riley epitomised a not uncommon reaction when he claimed that no 'poetic import can be claimed for the book', and railed against 'a new audience for poetry, one which must be presumed to have previously fought shy of it as too difficult or too deep'.[5] Certainly, it is not a work of avant garde complexity, but Cope's debut is not as cosily complacent, nor 'easy', as such critics indicate. It is in fact highly allusive and resistant to orthodoxies – and was a thorn in the side of the literary and cultural establishment into which she was instantly propelled. This chapter assesses the ways in which Cope's debut collection is an ambivalent, nuanced, and parodic response to British institutions, and to the orthodoxies of the male-dominated literary world she was entering.

What is often overlooked is that the book begins with poems lampooning British institutions and customs, and often with serious critical intentions, gently yet insidiously antagonising the establishment. This subversive tendency is signalled to some extent in the first poem, 'Engineers' Corner', which makes a satirical stand against the marginalisation of poetry while simultaneously lambasting tweedy parochialism: 'the person who can write a sonnet / Has got it made' (*MC* 3), she writes, with an irony she couldn't then have known would grow double, as she went on to earn enough from her writing to give up her day job. 'That's why this country's going down the drain', it ends, the speaker embracing a kind of parochially conservative *Daily Mail* rhetoric about falling standards.

The book's second poem, 'All-Purpose Poem for State Occasions', broadens the assault by cheerily making a mockery of State-sanctioned boilerplate. Its speaker is the generic author of a British 'State' poem tapping into the fervour of an unquestioning public who behave as that State would want them to. The Poet Laureate John Betjeman had died in 1984, and the poem was a response to a subsequent BBC commission to write about the Laureateship.[6] When Betjeman's successor Ted Hughes died in 1998, Tony Harrison, a favourite to replace him, would publish the poem 'Laureate's Block', attacking the eventual successor Andrew Motion as 'Di-deifying Motion', and putting himself out of contention for a position he would 'never seek'.[7] Cope's poem, constructed from three limericks, uses mild satire rather than direct personal polemic, to ridicule the prospect of such poetic commitments:

> The nation rejoices or mourns
> As this happy or sombre day dawns.
> Our eyes will be wet
> As we sit round the set,
> Neglecting our flowerbeds and lawns. (*MC* 4)

While examples exist of poems comprising multiple limerick stanzas that do not ridicule, cajole, or vanish into ridiculousness, this is not one of them. Indeed, not only does it point up the rote tediousness of such tamely expectation-satisfying verse, it also highlights the kowtowing instincts of British people from 'Dundee and Penzance and Ealing' – Scottish, Cornish, English (and presumably Welsh) – keen to pretend they 'love every royal', and then to use such fervour as an excuse to 'drink till we're reeling'. The apparent incongruity of the poem's form, frequently used for silly and often offensive subject matter, is a tacit rebuke both to the sententiousness of poems commissioned to reinforce such institutions and behaviours, and (more gently), the blind fealty of much of the coach-class public who are 'British and loyal' but do not question why, or what might serve them best. It also implies something about the way such behaviour more properly might be treated.

The next poem, 'A Policeman's Lot', is then prefaced with an epigraph by then-Poet Laureate Ted Hughes: 'The progress of any writer is marked by those moments when he manages to outwit his own inner police system' (*MC* 5). This is surely made more difficult for a Laureate, in the service of patrons, who has effectively precluded himself from criticising those patrons or the system upholding them in his poetry, and there is some justification for the opinion of the critic A. Alvarez that Hughes's 'duties as Poet Laureate seemed to have got the better of him'.[8] Certainly, also, the epigraph and the mock-boilerplate 'State' poem immediately preceding it have contradicting speakers, the latter being an ironic epitome either of self-policing or the complete absence of independent thought. Like the speaker of 'All-Purpose Poem for State Occasions', the speaker of 'A Policeman's Lot' is in the service of the Crown, not of the art of poetry:

> Although it's disagreeable and stressful (bull and stressful)
> Attempting to avert poetic thought ('etic thought),
> I could boast of times when I have been successful (been successful)
> And conspiring compound epithets were caught ('thets were caught).

In a style lifted from 'The Sergeant's Song' from Gilbert and Sullivan's *The Pirates of Penzance*, Cope's policeman speaker is

Hughes's 'inner' policeman, 'Patrolling the unconscious' of the 'prolific blighter' responsible for such psychologically complex works as *The Hawk in the Rain* and *Crow,* and having a tough time. Richard Collins and James Purnell call this poem 'an irresistible guying of Hughes's sententiousness',[9] but for all its jocularity there is no implication that Cope disagrees with the words of Hughes's she uses as an epigraph. As in the song that it echoes, the ends of most lines are repeated in parentheses; when we read that 'the imagination of a writer (of a writer) / Is not the sort of beat a chap would choose (chap would choose)', we can almost imagine the parenthetical echoes coming not from a pack of British bobbies, as they are in 'The Sergeant's Song', but gleefully from Cope, from Hughes, from writers.

There is, then, a subtle implication, by dint of the poem's placement after Cope's dig at State-sanctioned poetry, that Hughes's 'subconscious' has been rendered a particularly difficult 'beat' due to his willingness to accept the Queen's shilling. Louise Tondeur suggests that the poem satirises 'the idea' expressed in Hughes's epigraph but, as much as that, in the context of its placing in *Making Cocoa for Kingsley Amis,* it satirises what might have been Hughes's unconscious at that time – and, through its ridiculous speaker, the officious British bobby on the beat and the system he upholds. As Tondeur goes on to note, a writer 'works best when s/he is not being watched by the "police system" or when the sense of being watched is sufficiently diminished',[10] and the poem gives that a specifically British context.

After three poems, then, *Making Cocoa for Kingsley Amis* has made a satirical stand against British institutions, which it also suggests are implicitly male (in 'Engineers' Corner', it is 'small boys' who do or do not 'dream of writing couplets / And spurn the bike, the lorry and the train'; her representative of the police is a 'chap'). The fourth poem, 'Reading Scheme', wittily shines a torch on the underbelly of dissatisfied family life, as well as sending up the Ladybird reading scheme Cope would have been familiar with through her work as a primary school teacher, a job she held for eighteen years.[11] This poem adopts the repetitive form of the villanelle (with some substitutions in the repetends), using them to imitate the word patterns of a children's instructional reader, and essentially functions as narrative that can be read two ways, offering different interpretations to innocence and experience, much like Sandro Del-Prete's optical illusion *Message d'Amour des Dauphins*.[12] The narrator is unreliably faux-naïve, and we must use our adult perspective to work out what is going on, which admittedly isn't difficult. Peter's and Jane's 'Mummy', who has 'baked a bun' – with all the connotative metaphorical weight of that phrase – has a visit from the milkman who 'likes mummy' – with all the connotative weight of that circumstance – and is interrupted by the return of 'Daddy in his car' (*MC* 7).

This villanelle constantly tempts us to see the speaker as an adult attempting child-speak: although monosyllabic, 'glum' (ascribed to the milkman after the car arrives) is too complex a synonym for 'sad' to fit the register; 'Has he a gun?' is an allusion beyond the remit of the educational reading scheme book (if not, for example, a cartoon); and the line 'Go Peter! Go Jane! Come, milkman, come!' is, for the initiated, a crude pun. The poem is a window on wholesale dissatisfaction in a world of kept-up appearances, and the two children whose experience it inhabits might be happy now, but only because of losable innocence. We see the world they can look forward to.

With their two tangoing repetends, villanelles are inherently suited to obsessional themes. 'Lonely Hearts' is another irreverent, pacey example of the form, which uses its repetitions to comment on the nature of a different sort of text: the newspaper lonely hearts column. The five three-line stanzas present five separate voices with needs at once bespoke and shared, in consecutive advertisements by people who inadvertently reveal wants beyond those that are romantic. These are: a male biker who 'seeks female for touring fun' and hence escapism; a gay vegetarian 'whose *friends* are few' (my emphasis); an exec who wants the liberating second youth provided by a 'bisexual woman, arty, young'; a 'Jewish lady with a son', who might have various religious and practical reasons to want support; and a Libran – the star sign most associated with a need for relationships[13] – who is 'blue' and, uniquely here, explicitly confesses his or her 'need' for companionship (*MC* 17). The repetends of 'Lonely Hearts' make insistent their speakers' various calls for love, and provide, in the context only of the column where their isolated needs are thrown together, a co-authored screed of longing, throughout which they repeat one another's phrases. These speakers are then brought together in the final stanza, where all share one voice, as well as one proxy home: 'Please write (with photo) to Box 152. / Who knows where it may lead once we've begun?'

Although not at all unsympathetic, 'Lonely Hearts' also contains a subtle dig at superficiality. We can assume none of the hopefuls provide photographs: lonely hearts columns, now superseded by Internet dating sites filled with detailed profiles, did not tend to allow for this, and none of the speakers of the poem promise to reciprocate. They all want more than they are able (or willing) to give. The same might also be said of the subject of the short and sharp 'At 3 a.m.', which more soberly addresses the subjects of the two villanelles discussed above. The poem contains two five-line stanzas, each describing a room and its occupants, separated by a single-line strophe. In the first, 'the room contains no sound / except the ticking of the clock', which becomes an objective correlative for the frantic isolation of the only person in it, the speaker (*MC* 20). Then, in the final stanza:

> Somewhere else
> you're sleeping
> and beside you there's a woman
> who is crying quietly
> so you won't wake.

There are three people in the poem, then, in two rooms, with one room described in each of the main, separated stanzas: we might be reminded that 'stanza' means 'room', and see the structure of the poem as form reflecting content. The second is finely balanced, with five lines shared evenly between a couple in bed, what Philip Larkin in 'Talking in Bed' terms 'An emblem of two people being honest'[14] – although of course in Cope's poem one of them is not being, and only he seems able to find the oblivion of sleep. Paradoxically, considering their contradictory desires, the two women in the poem (if we indulge a heteronormative reading) have more than this man in common.

The next poem, the 10-part sequence 'From June to December', concerns the throes of new love, and moves from naïve paean to bitter lesson. The title intimates a sort of year- and cycle-completing sequel to 'Januarie and May', the colloquial name often given to Chaucer's 'The Merchant's Tale', after its main characters,[15] and both narratives show the unhappy results of a more experienced man in a relationship with a less experienced woman – although in Cope's poem the balance of sympathies is reversed in favour of the woman, and she is the one who is duped. Cope's speaker seems desperate to throw herself in too deep too soon with an apparently self-consciously sophisticated man, whose self-avowed 'concern for the rights of women / Is especially welcome news' (*MC* 21). Ultimately, though, 'You failed to fall in love with me' and the lesson, expressed in the final part (another obsessive villanelle) is that 'It's easy for a man to win' (*MC* 24). Her resolve, in response, is to promise 'to be nice to you', while secretly 'hat[ing] you all the while' – a position ambivalently poised between rising above the situation, and subservience in the wake of exploitation (*MC* 25).

'On Finding an Old Photograph', another poem of self-doubt, is also about a loss of innocence and the pressures of a relationship between a man exuding experience and younger woman – here father and daughter. Seeing a photograph of her father in youth, when she was 'unborn',

> eases a burden
> made of all his sadness
> and the things I didn't give him. (*MC* 18)

Note that 'and': the father's 'sadness' when she knew him was inherent, although the speaker adds to it her own guilt. We can only surmise what those 'things' are (grandchildren? Love? Understanding?), but certainly the speaker blames herself while also giving us no sense that the father blamed her. The tone and subject of the poem are reminiscent of Charles Causley's 'Eden Rock', in which the speaker's dead parents 'beckon' him from the metaphorical 'other bank'[16] – but in Cope's poem the connection to a parent isn't ahead and (to those with commensurate faith) possible, but irrevocably behind, and only artificially available through a trick of celluloid.

The next poem, 'Tich Miller', then evokes the speaker's own youth, from being one of the 'last two / left standing' (besides the eponymous Tich) when teams were picked for games at primary school, to finding her place among a nerdier set at secondary school (*MC* 19). It ends:

> In time I learned to get my own back,
> Sneering at hockey-players who couldn't spell.
>
> Tich died when she was twelve.

That discordant slant rhyme, only the second end-rhyme in the poem and its first consecutive one, makes the simple declaration of the isolated last line jar, as we realise that, ultimately and in the most important of contexts, Tich was not 'left standing'.

Cope has said that Tich 'was not the real name of the girl' (*TCL* 87). Her pseudonym is a homophone of a diminutive, and calls to mind the protagonist of Philip Larkin's 'Sunny Prestatyn', 'Titch Thomas', who futilely attempts to bring an unfair world down to his level by vandalising a poster of a 'girl' with 'spread, breast-lifting arms' (Larkin, 64). Cope's more benign Tich never reached that age of disillusion, though, and has more in common with the boy in Wordsworth's 'The Prelude' who 'was taken from his mates, and died / In childhood, ere he was full twelve years old',[17] which the last line of Cope's poem echoes – though, of course, Tich had no friends. The 'two duds' of her poem were never a pair, never confidantes, but individuals thrown together awkwardly because both lacked something (much like the speakers of 'Lonely Hearts'), before being set to work ineffectively in opposition.

'Emily Dickinson', the only other poem in the collection named after a woman or girl and the sole poem to mention a female poet, also takes a troubled figure for protagonist, but has an entirely different timbre and focus. A few small metrical substitutions notwithstanding, the poem is a double dactyl: an inherently humorous eight-line poetic form, with two dactyls comprising each line, the first of which is a compound adjective (here 'higgledy-piggledy'), and the sixth a single word. After highlighting that Dickinson 'Liked to use dashes / Instead of full stops', Cope writes that 'Critics and editors' no longer tolerate such 'Idiosyncrasy' (*MC* 13). This is evidently a swipe at the proclivities of literary tastemakers and gatekeepers in her own time, about which Cope can be defensively offensive: in 'Manifesto' she takes aim at 'a bloodless literary fart' critic

(*MC* 32). However, the 'Nowadays' in 'Emily Dickinson' is a misfire, ignoring the fact that Dickinson's immense posthumous popularity was partly facilitated by the revolution of literary modernism, which has permitted such 'idiosyncrasy' of style to flourish.

Of course, the poem isn't a parody, most of which are in the second section of the book, and we shall come to them shortly. But three poems in the first section directly parody or toy with the poems or styles of two canonical poets: William Wordsworth and T. S. Eliot. The poet-subjects of her parodies and lampoons, all men, are without exception presented in po-faced fashion as comically pompous or sententious, and never more so than in 'A Nursery Rhyme as it might have been written by William Wordsworth'. However, as Andrew Bennett notes, this poem 'explores the pretensions of a certain idea of Wordsworth', rather than a more accurate version of the poet.[18] Like 'Emily Dickinson', it is happy to take for sport a not altogether true (or fair) stereotype about its poet-subject, in this case humourless wonder, in addition to formally echoing his predilection for solid, rhymed pentameters in order to make 'his' pronouncements all the more ludicrous. The misty-eyed, fell-wandering speaker remembers a chance encounter with a talking sheep, who 'broke the moorland peace / With his sad cry, a creature who did seem / The blackest thing that ever wore a fleece' (*MC* 8). Walking 'towards him on the stony track', the speaker 'asked him, "Have you wool upon your back?" / Thus he bespake: "Enough to fill three bags"'.

'Bespake' is cod-Wordsworthian, a comedic, decorous over-egging that does not appear in any of his poems.[19] So is the conversation with the sheep, and the poem's self-absorbed valedictory couplet: 'And oft, now years have passed and I am old, / I recollect with joy that inky pelt'. And yet this line does have a near-parallel in Wordsworth's 'The Oak and the Broom', in which a talking broom (gorse) bush is quoted thus:

> Beneath my shade the mother-ewe
> Lies with her infant lamb; I see
> The love, they to each other make,
> And the sweet joy, which they partake,
> It is a joy to me.[20]

Such bucolic whimsy and casual anthropomorphising is at odds with modern sensibilities, but it remained popular more than a century later, in the work of poets considerably less skilful than Wordsworth. Cope's poem also has a less obvious parallel text in William Kerr's artlessly grand, sentimental 'Counting Sheep':

> I lingered at a gate and talked
> A little with a lonely lamb.
> He told me of the great still night [...].
> Of how, when sheep grew old,
> As their faith told,
> They went without a pang
> To far green fields.[21]

So, Cope's and Kerr's poems are both ostensibly wistful (although sheep seem less sentimental than poets), and both have a solitary, presumably male, rural wanderer poet and a chatty sheep who passes on knowledge – although Kerr's is of the more familiar 'snow-white' variety. Kerr was one of the 'Georgian Poets', and the five *Georgian Poetry* anthologies (1912–22) sold in huge numbers. He and most other Georgians (with some very notable exceptions, such as Edward Thomas) have since fallen from view and acclaim, but he once took his place among the proportion of that almost-exclusively male, often sub-Wordsworthian coterie who briefly received more respect than they deserved, and who were not all above earnestly writing poems not incomparable to Cope's. Would her poem look out of place in one of the *Georgian Poetry* anthologies? Only just.

Facing this parody in a double-page spread, to make an unlikely pair, is 'A Nursery Rhyme as it might have been written by T. S. Eliot'. This poem begins with a simple backhanded pastiche of 'Burnt Norton', the first of Eliot's *Four Quartets*: 'Because time will not run backwards / Because time / Because time will not run' (*MC* 9), but here in the service of presenting a rendering of 'Hickory Dickory Dock'. While the previous parody evokes other poems and poets besides its main target, this one is as directly and intricately intertextual with its main target as it is ludicrously dismissive; the rest of the poem brings in allusions to Eliot's poems 'Preludes', *The Waste Land*, 'The Love Song of J. Alfred Prufrock', and 'The Hollow Men'. The most famous of her poems toying with Eliot, however, is 'Waste Land Limericks': a set of witty summaries of the five parts of *The Waste Land*, with a suitably truncated title: note the dropping of Eliot's definite article, the sort of move sure to upset a pedant, and indicative of her posturing. For example, the 139 lines of part iii, 'The Fire Sermon', are distilled to:

> The Thames runs, bottles rattle, rats creep;
> Tiresias fancies a peep –
> A typist is laid,
> A record is played –
> Wei la la. After this it gets deep. (*MC* 10)

Predictably, 'Waste Land Limericks' has been too much for some critics. In his aforementioned hatchet-wielding review, Peter Riley states that, in Cope's hands, *The Waste Land* 'can only be parodied by reducing [it] absurdly' (Riley, 79). Others seem to misunderstand what the poem is up to. The critic Marta Pérez Novales claims, 'This is obviously written by someone who finds Eliot's style ludicrous, and makes fun of it.'[22] However, unlike the second 'Nursery Rhyme', this poem doesn't draw on Eliot's style at all. 'Waste Land Limericks' is a retelling of a long masterpiece in a form wholly unsuited to it, pointedly devoid of stylistic nods to Eliot's poem. As William Logan puts it, the poem is a work of 'cunning insouciance':[23] the form and register are farcically inappropriate vehicles for any rendition of Eliot's poem. There are also parts of it that Cope's version 'insouciantly' misunderstands. For example, in the passage quoted above, Cope seems to suggest the 'Wei la la' is the noise of the superficial record Eliot's 'lovely woman [...] puts on the gramophone' in lines 253–6 of *The Waste Land*. Eliot's 'Weialala leia / Wallala leialala' in fact echoes the refrain contrasted with that in one of his sources, Wagner's opera *Götterdämmerung*, later in the poem, at lines 266–78 and 290–1.[24] Her butchering precis of it is performative ambivalence.

Part II of *Making Cocoa for Kingsley Amis* is dominated by her invented poet Jake Strugnell, a figure as ludicrous as Cope's versions of Wordsworth or Eliot, and as likely to misunderstand what he is up against as the speaker of 'Waste Land Limericks'. Some of the poems in this half of the book are expressly by 'him', and others are only 'Strugnell poems' by proximity to those.[25] Strugnell, from the unglamorous south London suburb of Tulse Hill, is a man in his forties (forty-three, according to '*From* Strugnell's Sonnets' (*MC* 50)) with a penchant for chasing women without success, aping the poetic styles of his more successful contemporaries, and self-aggrandisement alternating with grimly perspicacious moments of self-reflection. As such, through Strugnell, Cope is able both to parody her contemporary poets, and simultaneously humorously point out the privileges of an anguished archetype. He is a figure of fun, but also a socially advantaged man with the McGonagallian knack of only being good because he isn't. That he is himself a parody of a poet with very serious intentions (even if they are hard to take seriously), renders his poems in the style of others' imitations on his part. His parodic existence also simultaneously makes each of his poems a double parody – of a paradigm of male poesy, as well as of whatever that paradigm happens to be ripping off – and often prevents us from gleaning much about what Cope herself thinks of the aped poets, because 'she' didn't write them.

We are introduced to him in 'Mr Strugnell', one of the poems not explicitly presented to us as having been written by the man himself:

> 'This was Mr Strugnell's room', she'll say,
> And look down at the lumpy single bed.
> 'He stayed here up until he went away
> And kept his bicycle out in that shed.' (*MC* 35)

The poem shadows Philip Larkin's famous 'Mr Bleaney', with which it shares a stanza pattern and narratological trajectory – although Larkin's speaker is the new recipient of the erstwhile room of Mr Bleaney, whereas this speaker looks beyond the current occupant's present in a moment of grim prolepsis: the landlady will end the monologue imagined for her by saying that Mr Strugnell is now 'Enjoying perfect boredom up in Hull'. In a manner reminiscent of her 'Nursery Rhyme as it might have been written by T. S. Eliot', the poem is littered with ludicrous variants of lines and phrases from Larkin's poem, such as the daftly tautological third line above, a counterpart to Larkin's 'he stayed / The whole time he was the Bodies till / They moved him'.

Moreover, it conflates Strugnell's habits with those of Mr Bleaney's author, himself the poet most identified with the emotionally detached, unromantic, and domestic tropes of Movement poetics, which had dominated British poetry in the late 1950s and early 1960s. As Nicola Thompson summarises, 'Cope uses Movement methodology to subvert Movement ideology',[26] at least if we take 'Movement ideology' to stand pejoratively for stuffy, overwhelmingly male parochialism, and that use of 'Movement methodology' comprises content as well as form. In that first stanza, we learn of Strugnell's Larkinesque habits of riding a bicycle and sleeping in a single bed: Larkin lived alone most of his life and we soon gather that Strugnell is a not especially eligible bachelor. His desire for 'perfect boredom' in Hull alludes both to where Larkin lived for thirty years, and Larkin's poem 'Dockery and Son', which contains the line 'Life is first boredom, then fear', so at least Strugnell isn't yet heading for the worse of those two eventualities. In 'Mr Strugnell' we discover that, like Larkin, he works in a library (in Strugnell's case, the provincial branch at Norwood) and loves jazz – although this and the accompanying sound of his tapping foot had been 'a bore' to the landlady, which she took in her stride, whereas in Larkin's poem the male speaker is left 'Stuffing my ears with cotton wool to drown / the jabbering set' used by his landlady. We also find out that he 'had a funny turn in sixty-three / And ran round shouting "Yippee! It's begun"', although again this is a comedic misrepresentation, for in the Larkin poem it alludes to, 'Annus Mirabilis', a hangdog speaker laments that the apparent sexual liberation of 1963 was 'rather late for me' (Larkin, 90). We also learn that he likes 'John Betjeman very much indeed' – again, much like Larkin, who regarded Betjeman as the joint 'greatest living English poet'[27] – but also that he is a man who likes to read the work of men, dismissing Pam Ayres and Patience Strong as 'too highbrow', an indication that he hasn't bothered to read these not remotely high-brow authors (or that he is patronising his landlady). As such, 'Mr Strugnell' makes a composite caricature of both Larkin and his poem, pinning Strugnell to it, so that all three come out looking pathetic. He is a cut-price, pastiche Larkin.

The next poem, 'Budgie Finds His Voice', parodies Ted Hughes – or is a work of pale imitation, if we suspend our disbelief enough and accept its subtitle: 'From *The Life and Songs of the Budgie* by Jake Strugnell'. This echoes the full title of Hughes's 1972 collection *Crow: From the Life and Songs of the Crow*. So, Budgie might find his voice, but Strugnell only finds a bargain-basement version of someone else's. This poem's closest counterpart in *Crow* is 'That Moment', and much of the wit in Cope's poem is in its proximity to that text. Both are single sentences, with the main clause saved for a final, isolated line. Both describe an apocalyptic scene, with the last human gone (in Hughes's poem he appears to commit suicide), and only a bird left to pick over the ruins. Moreover, Cope/Strugnell replicates the construction and cadences, if crucially not the connotations or gravity, of Hughes's images. Hughes's poem begins:

> When the pistol muzzle oozing blue vapour
> Was lifted away
> Like a cigarette lifted from an ashtray [...].[28]

The second stanza of the Cope/Strugnell counterpart reads:

> When the sun was lifted away
> Like an orange lifted from a fruit bowl [...]. (*MC* 37)

Gone is the delayed rhyme, the delay caused by the enjambments of Hughes's second line, the comparison of things ostensibly alike and uncannily different in purpose. Instead, Cope/Strugnell makes the huge bathetically insignificant, the sun becoming a piece of fruit. Likewise, the body in Hughes's poem, prone 'on the gravel / Of the abandoned world', is replaced with the implausibly solitary 'last ear on earth' that 'lay on the beach / Deaf'. But the biggest dose of bathos is saved for the final line. Hughes ends with 'Crow had to start searching for something to eat': Crow carries on, dispassionately. So does Budgie: '"Who's a pretty boy then?" Budgie cried'. Like Strugnell the failed poet, Budgie is left mindlessly professing his superficial worth to nobody.

To what extent is Cope dismissing her lauded male peers, such as Eliot, Larkin, and Hughes? As Henry King has pointed out,

Cope's parodies 'aren't simple lampoons: they imply the respect necessary to such telling imitations'.[29] She recalled beginning to write poems after teaching Ted Hughes,[30] has said that some of her earliest attempts were 'poor imitations of T. S. Eliot',[31] and has described Larkin's poetry as having 'knocked me sideways'.[32] Another poet she admired, and parodied, was Craig Raine, the editor of her first book.[33] Raine was hugely famous at that time for his 'Martian' poems, which are thick with unusual similes – making him at the time almost, at least superficially, the contemporary metaphysical poet. His own debut collection, *The Onion, Memory* (1978), opens with a section called 'Yellow Pages', comprising seven poems about the working lives of men engaged in the sort of manual labour Raine had no need to do, such as 'The Butcher', 'The Gardener', and 'The Window Cleaner'.[34] In this context, Cope's solemn focus in 'The Lavatory Attendant', on the dismayed lot of a man with one of the least glamorous jobs going, can be regarded as a pointed ratcheting up of commensurate affectation. He is pictured, sententiously, not as an overall-wearing bloke in the loos, but as a man of the cloth, in 'sacerdotal white', guarding 'a row of fonts // With lids like eye-patches' (*MC* 39), and this sub-metaphysical conceit is a blatant mockery of those favoured at the time by Raine. At the end of a day of mopping up after 'Short-lived Niagaras', he symbolically – although only symbolically – equalises his servitude: 'He turns Medusa on her head / And wipes the floor with her'.

This poem sits second in a run of four poems also parodying Peter Porter, Seamus Heaney, and Geoffrey Hill. These are not attributed to Strugnell, although as they are in the section in which work bearing his name appears it is hard not to see him in them, and Cope has left us unable to be sure either way. What follows these, however, is certainly a parody refracted through her bard of Tulse Hill. With its simple refrain of love and yearning, 'thinking of you', repeated five times across nine lines over the space of two pages, 'Strugnell in Liverpool' finds Strugnell playing at being the popular Liverpool poet Adrian Henri, who litters his 1969 book-length poem *City* with the same phrase.

Henri's frenetic poem is full of quotidian narratives, memories, and ephemeral consumer goods, punctuated by the constant of an absent 'you':

thinking of you

coming home

cat waiting black bigeyed in the hall
for Kit-E-Kat

going out again

leaving her rolled up sleeping
warm catdreams on the settee

thinking of you
thinking of you[35]

'Strugnell in Liverpool' tells the ostensibly comparable 'story' of Strugnell's solitary morning: waking alone, going naked to the toilet, getting dressed, and then thinking of the 'pink / nylon panties', 'blue / nylon bra', and 'white / nylon panties' of the object of his apparent devotion (*MC* 42–3). Those brash enjambments, and the many others throughout the poem, clearly evoke Henri's heavily enjambed switchbacks of thought and impression, with the caveat that Strugnell reveals his limitations by artlessly cutting through syntactical units rather than laying them one below the other as Henri tends to. He is a bad imitator, and the joke is on him more than on Henri. Like Henri and the other poets who appeared with him in the phenomenally popular anthology *The Mersey Sound* (1967), Roger McGough and Brian Patten, his poem is also scattered with low-brow references, normally to branded goods – although what he is doing 'alone in the toilet' (aren't we usually?) with 'the Andrex / thinking of you' might be given away by him then immediately 'eating my cornflakes', which were invented to dissuade 'troubled masturbators from the sinful act'.[36] As with 'Budgie Finds His Voice', the poem simultaneously shows Strugnell desperate to cling to the coat-tails of a more popular contemporary, thereby finding no voice of his own, and revealing more about his tendencies than he might have intended.[37]

'God and the Jolly Bored Bog-Mouse' ramps up Strugnell's proclivity for imitation. The poem is subtitled 'Strugnell's entry for the Arvon/*Observer* Poetry Competition 1980. The competition was judged by Ted Hughes, Philip Larkin, Seamus Heaney and

Charles Causley' – an all-male line-up almost unthinkable now. True to form, Strugnell provides a poem at once banal and derivative, and does so in a manner that inadvertently ridicules his intended audience of judges in an attempt to suck up to them. Each of the poem's four stanzas follows the same pattern of derivations. This is the third:

> Mouse dreamed a Universe of Blood,
> He dreamed a shabby room,
> He dreamed a dank hole in the earth,
> (back to the jolly womb). (*MC* 45)

The first lines of each stanza, then, echo Hughes (here, *Crow*, again), the second Larkin (here, 'Mr Bleaney', again), and the third Heaney (here, the 'bog poems' mainly collected in his 1975 collection *North*).[38] The poem is in ballad stanzas, a form favoured by Causley, and the fourth lines, each containing the word 'jolly', call to mind Causley's 'I Saw a Jolly Hunter', in which the word is repeated with increasingly bitter implications in almost every line (Causley, 215). Again, as we work through his bizarre narrative yoking together clichéd versions of their different sensibilities and styles, it is clear the joke is on Strugnell and other poets with comparable motivations, more than on the poets 'he' emulates so feebly.

'God and the Jolly Bored Bog-Mouse' is followed by the longest piece in the book, although we are encouraged to believe that it is in fact only an excerpt. '*From* Strugnell's Sonnets' provides poems 'i' to 'vii' in the sequence, although given the length of sequences by his Renaissance models, who knows how long Strugnell might go on for?[39] Thematically, the sequence is a base equivalent of most of its Renaissance counterparts, concerned as it is with a form of love-longing for an absent flame – satirising 'men who never outgrow the self-centred and gloomy sexual fixations of adolescence', as Timothy Steele puts it.[40] Each section is a Shakespearean sonnet, and begins with a line, often slightly altered, from the start of one of Shakespeare's, although not its corresponding number. Thus, in the first, the start of Shakespeare's 'Sonnet 129', 'Th' expense of spirit in a waste of shame / Is lust in action'[41] becomes 'The expense of spirits is a crying shame', and Shakespeare's analysis of the pursuit, experience, and memory of lustful passion is, in a pun on 'spirit', reduced to a lament that women are out of reach because they like expensive drinks and won't 'come across on half a pint of beer' (*MC* 46). We might be reminded of U. A. Fanthorpe's famous poem 'Not My Best Side', an ekphrastic parody of the legend of George and the Dragon, in which an equally belligerent male warns the damsel against 'being choosy', and reveals his narrow ambitions, sense of entitlement, and sad vulnerability.[42]

This rather sets the tone for the whole (excerpt of the) sequence. The second sonnet begins with the opening line of Shakespeare's 'Sonnet 14', 'Not from the stars do I my judgement pluck' (Shakespeare, 139), although whereas Shakespeare's speaker rejects astrology, Strugnell has read his horoscope for the day and readily accepts its promise of 'luck / With money and girls' (*MC* 47), the first of which would apparently have solved his problem with the second in the opening sonnet. The end of the poem is less Sidney's *Astrophel and Stella* – star-gazer and star – than horoscope-gazer and mirror: Cancerians 'make fantastic lovers, warm and gentle', although it is 'Amazing' that the object of his devotion fails 'to see / How very well all this applies to me'. Then, in 'iii', we learn that he turned to writing poetry in an attempt to win her and other women round, in the belief they 'love a bard, however dire, / And overlook my paunch because I write' (*MC* 48) – although they don't, as the second sonnet has revealed.

Sonnet 'iv' then turns from Shakespeare's 'Sonnet 55' (Shakespeare, 221) to 'Sonnet 18' (Shakespeare, 147), to end with an uncharacteristic moment of less vainglorious self-reflection: 'your beauty and my name will be forgotten – / My love is true, but all my verse is rotten' (*MC* 49). He writes poems, of all things, for what they might bring him now in love and riches, with no delusory eye on posterity. In 'v', we gather that Strugnell lost the presumably younger object of his affections when his musical tastes reminded her of her father's, and 'vi' begins with a bitter counterpart to the opening of Shakespeare's 'Sonnet 116' (Shakespeare, 343): 'Let me not to the marriage of true swine / Admit impediments' (*MC* 51), in which the meaning of 'admit' shifts from 'let in' in Shakespeare's poem, to 'concede' in Strugnell's. She has gone off with a new man and his 'big car', leaving Strugnell to dedicate himself to the 'Higher Things' for which he has already made plain he doesn't intrinsically care. It ends:

> One day I'll make my mark,
> Although I'm not from Ulster of from Mars,
> And when I'm published in some classy mag
> You'll rue the day you scarpered in his jag.

It is as though Strugnell has read 'Engineers' Corner' and taken it at face value. Again, Cope (through Strugnell) swipes playfully at some of her largely male contemporaries, at a time when several poets in Northern Ireland, such as Heaney, Michael Longley, and Derek Mahon, were popular and often writing about the ongoing Troubles, and the aforementioned 'Martian poets' such as Raine and Christopher Reid were in their first flush of popularity. Unfortunately for Strugnell, Tulse Hill just isn't very exciting, and the literary greatness he seeks for non-artistic reasons remains a pipe dream as he advances through middle age and farther off the radar of the young women who will never become less alluring to him.

The final sonnet presents Strugnell meditating bitterly on using poetry to vanish into misanthropic solipsism. However, in true Strugnellian fashion, that isn't achieved by absorbing himself in poetry, but by using a book of it as a dull siren to warn people off talking to him during a train journey. If he has learned anything, it seems, it is that poetry won't get him the girl, and might in fact make him a pariah, and by now he has given up enough to embrace that reality. Again, he (and she) takes aim at a famous male contemporary of whom Strugnell and his ilk would be monumentally jealous:

> Recent research in railway sociology
> Shows it's best to read the stuff aloud:
> A few choice bits from Motion's new anthology
> And you'll be lonelier than any cloud. (*MC* 52)

As István D. Rácz has noted, 'support and subversion coexist in her Strugnell poems'.[43] This anthology can only be *The Penguin Book of Contemporary British Poetry*, edited by Andrew Motion and her former poetry tutor Blake Morrison.[44] In addition to including some of Motion's own poetry, it contains work by two of the poets parodied in *Making Cocoa for Kinglsey Amis*, Seamus Heaney and Craig Raine, and has often been criticised for its perceived parochialism and inclusion of Irish poets – neither of which are Strugnell's concerns, of course.[45] We might fairly assume that the rest of 'Strugnell's Sonnets' slip increasingly into the vortex of his navel; Cope spares us the details.[46]

The book's second section ends with Strugnell's attempts at minimalism, as this antithesis of a Zen sensibility turns his hand to haiku. The first of the three 'Strugnell's Haiku' reads:

> The cherry blossom
> In my neighbour's garden – Oh!
> It looks really nice. (*MC* 55)

True to the expectations of the form, we have the syllabic constraint, two natural images, the evocation of a season; true to Strugnell, the poems vanish into bathos in the first, self-obsession in the second (in which 'my hair also' falls), and baser desires in the third ('pubs are open'). Here, at least for this collection, we leave him, sure that his sudden interest in brevity is not a sign he is about to give up altogether on his bardic dreams. As we shall see, Cope's next collection, *Serious Concerns*, would prove otherwise. Strugnell was too useful a stooge for needling her contemporary poetic culture.

Then, in a final twist, Cope wittingly and wittily undermines herself again. The book's last poem, given added prominence by being separated alone in section III, is the four-line title poem, 'Making Cocoa for Kingsley Amis'. The title was apparently a 'dream', a record of which 'seemed vital', even though it 'wouldn't be much of a poem' (*MC* 59). There is something comically irreverent about making this the title poem. It seems the move of a poet who refuses to take herself too seriously – or perhaps seriously enough. If we take the speaker to be Cope, and nothing suggests otherwise, it is also a poem in which a woman, in the unwilled subconscious of dreaming, serves a man.

At the end of the collection, then, she records the 'vital' dream that playfully undermines all the book's subtle and less subtle jibes at gendered habits and adherence to traditional gender roles. In 'My Lover', earlier in the collection, she celebrates a partner for minor acts of selflessness and devotion, including, among other things, making her 'smooth cocoa'; contrastingly, in the final poem, she envisages making cocoa for a man. Doing so is therefore perhaps also symbolic of a sense of literary hierarchy: Cope was yet to publish a book when she wrote it, and in the year she did, Amis won the Booker Prize for his nineteenth novel (excluding one that was co-authored and another published under a pseudonym), *The Old Devils*. Amis, a great comic writer, can be seen to represent an aspiration, and a dream about making him cocoa can, by perhaps an over-enthusiastic extension, be regarded as a displacement of her subconscious and conscious desire to emulate. At any rate, despite, in Christopher Reid's words, 'ruthlessly mocking literary pretentions and absurdities',[47] the book ends doing what it has done so many times already: paying a kind of homage to a literary hero without kowtowing. *Making Cocoa for Kingsley Amis* implicitly asks where a woman can fit into this overwhelmingly male tradition. Moreover, in answering not only with biting, nuanced, and layered parodies, but with direct poems of love and longing that have become part of that tradition, it offers a riposte to Amis's assertion in his poem 'A Bookshop Idyll' that, whereas men can 'get by without' love, 'Women don't seem to think that's good enough – / They write about it'.[48] Yes, they do – or at least this one does – and in a final, playful, act of apparent revenge, she eponymously dedicated her book to him.[49] Her next collection might have carried Amis's words as an epigraph.

2

'He thinks you're crazy': *Serious Concerns* (1992)

Serious Concerns appeared six years after Cope's debut, and was equally successful, selling more than 180,000 copies by 2008.[1] It is, however, a far unhappier collection: true, as Thomas Sutcliffe has put it, 'not just to the feelings you feel you should be feeling, but to those you actually are'.[2] The book is in six numbered sections, but the distinctions between them are soft, the dominant moods transmuting rather than quantum leaping as one reads. Nonetheless, the focus shifts throughout, from frustrated romance, to the mocking of pretensions (although that remains a constant – as Julie Kane has noted, Cope is 'always ready to plunge a sharp pen into the balloon of anyone's pretentiousness'),[3] back to frustrated romance, and on to a release of love and its concomitant contemplations. The 'serious concerns' of the book are several, and in some cases the collection's title gives the poems a delightfully ironic edge, as we shall see. Prime among them, however, is the serious concern of loneliness, most often wrapped in a protective shell of ostensibly anti-male gallows humour.

Cope has said, 'When I started writing, women poets [...] were very much in the minority and I felt there wasn't much encouragement for women to tell it how it is about what happens between men and women.'[4] She has also described her diaries from the time she was writing the poems for her second book, and living alone in London, as 'like Bridget Jones on speed',[5] so it is no surprise that this influenced the direction of her poetry. Whereas *Making Cocoa for Kingsley Amis* had focused on many male poets, *Serious Concerns* turned its lens more concentratedly to a version of men being from Mars and women being from

Venus, and the desperate personal struggle to get them into alignment.

'Bloody Men', the opening poem and one of her most popular,[6] draws on the saying – often used as a metaphorical adage – that you wait ages for a bus and then three come along at once. 'Bloody men are like bloody buses' because after 'about a year' of waiting, you'll be bamboozled by several all at once 'Offering you a ride' (*SC* 3). We probably shouldn't fail to notice that buses are designed to take a great many people 'for a ride', without any motivation beyond a transaction, which makes this a rather hyperbolic poem about the apparent hopelessness of relationships, at least if we take the simile to its conclusion.[7] However, this poem, in three ballad stanzas, is partnered over the page – like the obverse of a coin – by another with the same form and an utterly different timbre. In 'Flowers', a suitor 'nearly bought me flowers':

> It made me smile and hug you then.
> Now I can only smile.
> But, look, the flowers you nearly bought
> Have lasted all this while. (*SC* 4)

It is not possible to 'look' at these never-existing flowers: that word pertains to the poem, and its attempt to immortalise their near-materialisation. In any case, had the flowers been bought, they would've perished long ago. This draws on another common saying: that it is the thought that counts – or, by extension, the memory. And this memory is cherished because it speaks to a temperamental connection between two people, both inclined to be tentative because of 'doubts – / The sort that minds like ours / Dream up incessantly'.

However, 'Now I can only smile': the other person is no longer there to hug. Again, love apparently didn't last: the speaker is off this bus.[8] As she puts it in 'The Aerial', which like 'Bloody Men' implies three potential lovers in close succession and then a long wait, 'Love came along. Love came along. / Then you. And now it's ended' (*SC* 6). But 'The Aerial' ends with a simple resolution to 'tidy up / And get the radio mended', sailing close to another idiomatic phrase: to make do and mend. It is a small gesture, but one symbolic of fortitude.

It also implies a desire to replace unpredictable company at close quarters with reliable company at a distance, that one can turn on and off. Between 'Flowers' and 'The Aerial' in the collection is 'Defining the Problem', which does what its title promises, and the conclusion is bleak: 'I cannot cure myself of love / for what I thought you were before I knew you' (*SC* 5). This bitter little quatrain poem, which reads like a coda to the sequence 'From June to December' (*MC* 21–5), suggests that the addiction of love is rooted in our quixotic notion that someone is perfect when he or she hasn't yet proven otherwise, and is destined to fail for precisely the same reason, landing us back at a desperate and hopeful square one.

This initial onslaught of losses in love – variously bitter, wistful, and resigned in those first four poems – is suddenly interrupted in 'The Orange', yet another three-stanza poem in ballad metre, in which the speaker shares 'a huge orange' with colleagues, then relishes the quotidian 'jobs on my list' (*SC* 7). This is a poem about renewed vigour to get things done because you feel loved and, crucially, have an outlet for the love you long to give; it also indicates an emotional upturn in fortunes simultaneously instigating productivity and lowering anxiety:

> And that orange, it made me so happy,
> As ordinary things often do
> Just lately. The shopping. A walk in the park.
> This is peace and contentment. It's new.

The harsh enjambment in the middle of this middle stanza, and therefore at the heart of the poem, is the only enjambment of a phrase in a poem of almost exclusively end-stopped lines, signalling the sudden realisation of the new phenomenon of 'contentment', this ability to evaluate positively her current circumstances. The staccato sentences that follow – eight in under six lines, ending 'I love you. I'm glad I exist.' – then slow the poem down, as though to cherish that realisation. In 'The Self-Unseeing', Thomas Hardy writes, 'Everything glowed with a gleam; / Yet we were looking away!';[9] Cope's speaker, on the other hand, has the privilege of full cognisance. The poem is presented as a suddenly found, hard-won release from the disappointment of the four poems preceding it.

In any case, the opening five poems of *Serious Concerns*, with their consistent voice and insistent thematic unity, suggest a speaker in a state of romantic and emotional instability. We might diagnose a need for therapeutic analysis. Cope had, in fact, been in therapy for as long as she had been a poet: as she put it in 2019, 'Writing poetry started about six months after I was in analysis, and I was getting in touch with feelings I needed to express' (*Desert Island Discs*). Her debut collection was dedicated to her therapist, Arthur S. Couch, but for all that book's desire to explore very strong feelings of both personal and public kinds, it had nothing explicit to say about therapy. *Serious Concerns*, on the other hand, contains three poems mentioning 'the shrink' and outlining apparent experiences had while seeing him. They imply therapy is not a quick fix, even while it involves the learning of hard truths. 'The Shrink', the first part of the two-part 'Two Hand-Rhymes for Grown-ups',[10] concludes:

> He thinks you're crazy,
> A nervous wreck.
> Say, 'Thank you, doctor',
> And write the cheque. (*SC* 29)

The diagnosis doesn't seem to help – certainly not as much as the cheque might help the 'shrink' – and presumably the speaker has only taken herself to see him because she already has concerns about her mental well-being. In 'As Sweet', addressed to a lover, she ends by sharing her therapist's conclusion that this man to whom she professes being 'so alike' is, rather less romantically, a 'narcissistic object-choice': Freudian jargon denoting 'one whose function is to maintain the cohesiveness, stability and positive affective colouring of the self-representation'.[11] Again, a diagnosis hardly seems to help in providing a cure; certainly, the bitter joke is that being told this can't do much to make the patient feel better, not least when she cries 'I long to see you, hear your voice' and finds herself confronted by (and confronting her lover, the addressee, with) the professionally-stated possibility that her feelings for him are not as 'true' as the poem has already promised.[12]

The poem preceding this, 'Some More Light Verse', is written in jaunty rhymed couplets of tetrameter, a favoured form for comic poems,[13] but form and content are cynically out of sync. The poem comprises two ten-line stanzas, split into thirty-five frantically staccato sentences, each stanza listing a repetitive litany of apparently futile self-improvement tasks:

> You have to try. You see a shrink.
> You learn a lot. You read. You think.
> You struggle to improve your looks.
> You meet some men. You write some books. [...]
> And nothing works. The outlook's grim. (*SC* 8)

As Mark Oakley points out, this poem 'captures the almosts and the absences that are more than capable of directing our lives', its speaker 'stuck with the difference between what things are and what they might have been'.[14] Seeing 'a shrink' in the first stanza becomes seeing 'the shrink' in the second, the movement from indefinite to definite article implying that though that habit solidifies, nothing seems to improve. Rather, the speaker is tantalised and tortured by apparently possible salves for unhappiness that turn out to be achingly futile. To reinforce that point, the last of the lines quoted above, which is also the only line in the poem not to include at least one stated attempt at self-improvement or securing happiness, appears verbatim in both stanzas. Moreover, the only set of four rhymes in the poem runs 'cry', try', and 'sigh', before repeating 'try' as the poem's last word, and leaving another that would make semantic sense, 'die', unsaid. Despite its ostensibly cheery tone, then, this despairing if tenacious poem is anything but light verse. It is rooted in despair, with form working hard against content.

Meeting 'some men' isn't likely to do much for your happiness if you can't stand the men you meet. While the first section of the book brims with poems of despair at failed relationships, the vagaries of the dating game, and the apparently futile dependence on therapy, its penultimate section contains several poems lambasting 'Men and Their Boring Arguments', as one poem title puts it, neatly summarising the poem beneath (*SC* 66). 'I Worry', from the same section, begins with apparent 'serious concern' at a man's feelings 'since we spoke', although the final stanza reveals that the speaker's concern is less charitable than we might have expected:

They say men suffer,
As badly, as long.
I worry, I worry,
In case they are wrong. (*SC* 67)

This perhaps reveals a more morally compromised desire for a 'narcissistic object-choice'. More likely, it is the bitter *cri de cœur* of the lovelorn.

'Advice to Young Women' rejects vengefulness in favour of fatalism, and is bitter and salutary: whether you 'wed in a hurry' and risk making the wrong choice, or wait and suddenly find yourself left to choose between 'husbands inclined to be naughty / And divorcés obsessed with their kids', you will find that 'life is hell' (*SC* 69). It's a po-faced warning as hyperbolically misanthropic as that of Philip Larkin's 'This Be the Verse', with its warning that 'Man hands on misery to man. / It deepens like a coastal shelf', and makes it explicitly clear that man hands on misery to woman, too.[15] In the Shakespearean sonnet 'Faint Praise', a blazon of sorts,[16] the female speaker ostensibly seems to reconcile with having apparently made one of the wrong choices available to her:

Small men can be aggressive, people say,
But you are often genial and kind,
As long as you can have things all your way
And I comply, and do not speak my mind. (*SC* 65)

As Stephen Regan notes, this poem 'blatantly undermines the traditional associations of the sonnet with [...] extravagant admiration'.[17] It also turns the romantic blazon, so popular in the Renaissance, into an asteistic attack. One can remove the faux-naïve, positive spin on these lines and paraphrase them thus: 'You are small, and sometimes aggressive, even when you get your own way, and you hate it when I voice an opinion you don't share.' The speaker must be held partly responsible for not walking away from this apparently dreadful relationship, and when she writes 'Nobody's perfect', in the penultimate line, we might hope she has the perspicacity to question her own judgement. The poem leaves that unclear.

Many of Cope's poems about masculinity, especially in her earlier collections, are as serious as they are often funny, and show or describe men holding forth in self-satisfaction, often to the detriment of the speaker's happiness. Elsewhere in the book, Cope pokes fun at other 'serious concerns' in the form of acts of self-satisfied virtue. We might frequently be reminded of Yeats's warning that 'The best lack all conviction, while the worst / Are full of passionate intensity',[18] and encouraged to extend Yeats's specific insight into the Irish politics of the 1910s to serve as a maxim for general application. Marta Pérez Novales claims that Cope's 'use of parody is less pervasive' in *Serious Concerns* than in her debut,[19] but I would contend that it is in fact equally prevalent. The central difference is that in her second book she more frequently parodies the attitudes and mores of groups, rather than individual poets.

One of those groups is the green lobby, the subject of several delicious mockeries in the book's second section. Environmental 'serious concerns' were a fashionable if necessary cause in the late 1980s and early 1990s, as awareness increased about the human causes of matters such as devastating meteorological events, the thinning of the ozone layer, and rising sea levels.[20] This found its way into poetry with what later came to be called ecopoetry.[21] Cope does not deny the seriousness of these things by lampooning those most keen to signal sudden and often hypocritical concerns about them. In 'A Green Song', which can be sung to the tune of 'Ten Green Bottles', a bottle-bank visitor thinks 'we'll save the planet' while dropping in 'bags of bottles' that have 'Cleaned us out of cash', meaning that the speaker is happy to be an avid consumer of unnecessary products that require manufacture and create waste, and is therefore part of the problem (*SC* 20). In this poem, then, an undoubtedly serious concern, for all of us, is reduced to an almost meaningless but fervently signalled assuagement of guilt and responsibility. 'The Concerned Adolescent', the speaker of which is eponymous, is a sprawl of artlessly overblown free verse railing against 'HUMAN BEINGS' who 'pollute the world', do not live 'in peace and love', and, crucially, 'do not see how important my poem is' (*SC* 21–2), making this speaker sound a lot like Strugnell in sonnet vi in '*From* Strugnell's Sonnets' (*MC* 51).[22]

The adolescent poet is immediately followed in *Serious Concerns* by our reacquaintance with the work of her invented poet *manqué* Strugnell, her late-middle-aged bard of Tulse Hill,

London, who less forgivably jumps on the same bandwagon with the suitably ludicrous and bathetic three-page 'Goldfish Nation'. It begins:

In the pond
There are no bombs, no guns, no bullets.
There is no property and no television.
The pond is the territory not of humans
But of the goldfish.
He is better than you. (*SC* 23)

How Strugnell is able to gender the goldfish we are not told, although it is perhaps characteristic of the unthinking chauvinist we have come to know in *Making Cocoa for Kingsley Amis* that he would designate the creature thus. Note also Strugnell's use of 'you', rather than 'us': like the 'concerned adolescent', Strugnell is sententious enough to think he writes from a unique position of virtue, that his 'serious concern' does not encompass a need to look at himself. As in some of his poems in Cope's previous book, here he inadvertently reveals his own failings and prejudices with comical regularity:

Goldfish are disinclined
To get into an argument.
They do not discuss interest rates
Or debate the ordination of women. (*SC* 25)

On the last point, we can surmise Strugnell's position.[23] In other respects, this could be read as the response of the 'small man' to the events recalled in the passage quoted from 'Faint Praise' earlier in this chapter.

It is easy to miss now, but the poem is a parody of the once phenomenally popular *Whale Nation* by the political activist and writer Heathcoat Williams, a book-length poem about whales, its languid lines of loose free verse interspersed with factual information.[24] 'Goldfish Nation' also contains factual information about goldfish – nothing her poem says about their behaviour is untrue – and towards the end she makes tangential reference to Williams's poem by writing that goldfish sex life 'is somewhat less exciting / than the mating of whales'. 'Strugnell' has simply taken Williams's style and adapted it to a banal subject, thereby allowing Cope to mock the sententiousness of the original poem and of those who would ape it in one fell swoop – and, by its proximity in the book to 'The Concerned Adolescent', also implying a link between Williams's admirers and modish, banal if well-meaning youth. In a sense it is more cutting than any of the Strugnell parodies in her debut collection, because here Strugnell doesn't really add much banality of his own to what he apes, other than a change of subject. The poem doesn't imply much respect for Williams's project.

Serious Concerns contains five poems by or about Strugnell, the sole recurring poetic character in her published work. This is fewer than in her debut, but a significant run, including two sequences of respectively three and four sections, and the three-page 'Goldfish Nation'. However, whereas in *Making Cocoa with Kingsley Amis* he is Jake Strugnell, in this book he is renamed Jason. It is perhaps excessive to read much into the change of name, although two possibilities come to mind, neither of which excludes the other. First, the change of name is a knowing reminder that Strugnell is an invention of Cope's, with her own double-bluffing voice behind it. Second, in the six years between her first two books, the Australian Jason Donovan had become the most famous dreamy-eyed pop boy in Britain, his first name synonymous with a sort of artistry, and easy success, comically at odds with the bard of Tulse Hill. We might imagine Strugnell has changed his own name in a ridiculous attempt to remain as relevant as possible to the young women he is so desperate to impress, such as his love targets in '*From* Strugnell's Sonnets' (*MC* 46–52).[25]

In keeping with 'Goldfish Nation', however, the Strugnell poems in *Serious Concerns* avoid love-longing and instead generally present self-serving impulses dressed up as noble ideals or attempts at new modes of poetic expression. The first of the three 'Strugnell's Christian Songs', which is 'sung to the tune of *Daisy Bell*', advocates being 'on Jesus' side', because those who are will 'get to heaven' and 'be winners who never died!' (*SC* 59). The original song, about love, hope, doubt, and a wish for matrimony is considerably closer to Christian thought than Strugnell's first foray into spiritual verse. In the poem's second section, which comprises a chain of five limericks and is therefore as formally unsuitable to its subject as is 'Waste Land Limericks' (*MC* 10), Strugnell expresses joy at his sudden discovery of Jesus, who keeps him 'calm and happy' (*SC* 60). Through Strugnell, Cope implies something about the self-satisfaction and knowing certainty now of the proselytiser, rather than the fair-weather ecologist. When mocked in the pub for toasting to Jesus,

> I muttered 'Just you wait
> Till you get to Heaven's Gate,
> You jerk.' Then I went back to being meek.

Of course, meekness isn't compatible with judgemental certainty about matters unproven, and Strugnell is not alone in failing to realise it.

Another piece 'by Jason Strugnell', 'Ahead of My Time', is a sequence of four short 'poems for musical performance', and essentially comprises directions for that performance (*SC* 57–8). It is anything but ahead of its time, and finds Strugnell coming many decades late to the avant garde fashion for group performance-based sound poetry. However, the opening section, 'Clouds', in which the performers are to pretend to be 'raining', feels more like a protracted and unenjoyable version of a primary school participation exercise. The second and third parts, 'Perplexity' and 'Weltschmerz', are consciously dominated by bewilderment and boredom, respectively:

> At irregular intervals
> scratch your head.
> ('Perplexity')

> When the tedium
> has become unbearable
>
> scream
> ('Weltschmerz')

'Weltschmerz' is German for a feeling of melancholy and world-weariness; while there is no direct counterpart for the word in English, it is evidently rather pretentious of Strugnell to rely on a word from another language we have no reason to believe, from his other poems or the actions implied by them, he would have learned to speak. The not-so-hidden implication of these middle sections is that they not only echo Strugnell's understanding of the medium he is currently struggling to master, they also mirror what an audience of such work might be inclined to do if it was honest with itself. By the fourth and final section, 'Quartet for Four Beer-Drinkers', Strugnell has hit upon the notion of marrying artistic creation with one of his favoured leisure pursuits:

> Take a swig of beer
> whenever you feel like it
> [...]
> Continue
> until all four glasses are empty

In other words, let drinking take precedence, then give up on the poem entirely. Again, Strugnell's subconscious and less artful desires bleed through the page; at least the audience will not be presumed to have to endure a long performance.

Strugnell's sequence can be seen as a sorry counterpart to works such as Jerome Rothenberg's *Technicians of the Sacred* (1968), an influential collection of poetry, chants and songs from native traditions in various parts of the world.[26] The Beat poets had also experimented with group performance and participatory poems, often with improvised parts, and this had been taken up by British poets such as Bob Cobbing in the 1970s: Cobbing's groups Bird Yak and Konkrete Canticle collaborated with other artists, and inspired similar collaborative projects among the avant garde British Poetry Revival.[27] Some Beats, such as Allen Ginsberg, were fabled for their supposedly debauched lifestyles, to which Strugnell's apparent obsession in his poem with downing a few pints seems a suitably tame counterpart.

No Strugnell poems from *Serious Concerns* were included by Cope in *Two Cures for Love: Selected Poems 1979–2006*, which contains seven poems attributed to Strugnell from her debut. This perhaps gives a clue to how she thought about her continuation of Strugnell's oeuvre, which then abruptly ended. Strugnell is a limited persona, if a special one, and the lampoons of his hapless character can only go so far. However, in the second collection, Strugnell's tendency to ape and lampoon his significant contemporaries is extended to a tendency to jump on board with contemporary trends, thereby allowing for the indirect lampooning of cultural tendencies as much as of individuals. The difficulty is that significant poets such as

Heaney and Larkin, who are victims of Strugnell poems in the first book, tend to remain relevant, whereas trends age, so the Strugnell poems in the latter collection are more likely to end up looking like time capsules, and have relatively diminished returns as time passes. One wonders, however, what Strugnell might do today to navigate self-promotion on social media, or to embrace identity politics in an effort to further his poetic ambitions. We are unlikely to find out, because in 2016 Cope claimed that the thought of writing another Strugnell poem 'depresse[s] me'. [28]

One poem in *Serious Concerns* gives an acronym for male poets – surely including but by no means limited to Strugnell. 'Tumps' stands for 'typically useless male poets', and in the poem of that name Cope suggests that her male counterparts are scatter-brained and lack the practical wherewithal to look after themselves properly: 'He probably can't drive a car / Or follow a map', and 'Don't let him loose on accounts' (*SC* 34). On the other hand,

> Women poets are businesslike, able,
> Good drivers, and right on the ball,
> And some of us still know our seven times table.
> We're not like the tumps. Not at all.

Methinks the lady doth protest too much, and certainly the last line rather over-states its case with the addition of that final sentence. This is part of the joke, of course, for earlier in the book, Cope's female speakers have shown themselves to be at times overwhelmingly troubled, distracted, and in need of support.

In any case, 'So Much Depends', which appears close to the end of the book's fifth and penultimate section, brings lovers, male poets (or at least poetry enthusiasts), men and their boring arguments, and apparent female practicality into constellation:

> I'll fight with you about important issues
> Like who should buy the bread or clean the sink
> But when it comes to William Carlos Williams,
> Dearest, I really don't mind what you think. (*SC* 72)

The poem takes for its title the opening words of Williams's 'The Red Wheelbarrow', an urgent, terse call to notice physical matters and their ineffable qualities.[29] That is utterly at odds with the conversation her poem evokes, and implies the male interlocutor hasn't understood much about at least that aspect of Williams's poetry. It is perhaps a surprise, then, that this vengefully witty book of dissatisfactions ends with several poems of renewed hope and contentment, largely revolving around feelings for a man: sitting back to 'think about the things you say and do / And nothing else' – note the emphasising enjambment – in 'On a Country Bus' (*SC* 80), or stepping out the door and feeling that 'I can go anywhere I choose' in 'New Season' (*SC* 83). The excited, suddenly satisfied tone of these poems has, of course, been presaged by 'The Orange' in the first section of the book, but a lot of spirited unhappiness has filled many of the intervening seventy pages.

These outpourings of joy and hope in the book's sixth and final section are, however, folded in among other poems where love is both tempered and exacerbated by the shortness of time – a theme that will become a leitmotif in Cope's later collections. In 'After the Lunch', saying goodbye precipitates for the speaker the uncomfortable acknowledgement – for it comes freighted with a sense of vulnerability – that 'I've fallen in love': 'On Waterloo Bridge with the wind in my hair / I am tempted to skip. *You're a fool.* I don't care' (*SC* 81). This poem's light anapaestic metre adds its spring to the speaker's steps. The italicised voice is that of her 'head' combatting her 'heart' with reason; but, ultimately, 'the heart is the boss', and hope wins out. The setting of this goodbye is intriguing, implying as it does that the speaker and subject are returning, respectively, to separate domains either side of the river. What connects them, like the bridge, is mutual feeling. It is potentially vulnerable, like a bridge, and can be swept away. We must trust it, all the same.

The following poem, 'In the Rhine Valley', shows a meeting of lovers tentatively embracing that mutual realisation:

> You're patient. You help me to learn
> And you smile as I practice the phrase,
> *'Die Farben der Baume sind schon.'* (*SC* 82)

This man's response is a long way from the responses of other men in the book, when a woman voices her opinion, such as the subject of 'Faint Praise' or the men in 'Men and Their Boring Arguments' who 'Don't give [women] a chance to begin' (*SC* 66). In any case, it seems that the relationship depicted in 'In the Rhine Valley' is conducted at distance, so time together is particularly precious:

> October. The year's on the turn –
> It will take us our separate ways
> But the sun shines. And we have two days.

Earlier in the book, 'Two Cures for Love' had offered the bitter advice that getting 'to know him better' is certain to solve that sickness (*SC* 68). Perhaps this is the case in 'In the Rhyne Valley', although certainly the poem brims with a newfound optimism that makes it appear the book's earlier bitterness has been left in the past, and the collection ends with the surprise hope of new love and happiness. The poem's ten lines tango around just two rhymes, distributed evenly: ABBABAABBA. This is two people in apparent synergy, as the poem is in prosodic synergy. And, like the poem, their time is short. This is made more potent by what is recognised in the line of German the speaker is trying to learn, which translates as 'The colours of the trees are beautiful'. Autumn colour is beautiful, but it is also a final flare of light before the closing in of winter.

The poem is a Chaucerian roundel: a version of the French repeating form, its first line repeated three times. In Cope's poem, that line is the German one, with its evocation of autumn. Chaucer's most famous lines in the form are contained near the end of his 699-line 'The Parliament of Fowls', in 'a roundel at here departynge', the repeated first line of which is 'Now welcome, somer, with thy sonne softe'.[30] This is one of the earliest poems to refer to Valentine's Day as a time for lovers. Cope's counterpart is aware of the beauty and transience of its moment, but there is also the suggestion that the future of not being together will also be transient, and might well then be replaced by a metaphorical, as well as literal, summer.

The book then ends with two elegies, followed by two poems about friends and family departing, all of which are moving in their directness. 'For My sister, Emigrating' has a Larkinesque trajectory, from the outlining of a circumstance to a philosophical conclusion:

> We never learn. We've grown up
> struggling, frightened
> that the family would drown us,
> only giving in to love
> when someone's dead or gone. (*SC* 86)

That last line is loaded, of course, coming as it does at the end of a poem following several others about learning to love and cherish the moment. Again, it is a conclusion reminiscent of Thomas Hardy's final lines to 'The Self-Unseeing', although 'In the Rhine Valley' has demonstrated a determination to cherish the moment, and look to the future. Remembering that is perhaps the most serious concern of them all.

3

'Still warm, still warm': *If I Don't Know* (2001)

Writing before the publication of Cope's second collection, and in reference to her first, Nicola Thompson looked forward to 'a Cope collection made up of "very serious" and "intense" love poems'.[1] Up to a point, that is what *Serious Concerns* delivered, though the 'love' rarely seemed to have been found, even while it was written about obsessively. A few years later, Cope was turning in a new direction, both in life and in art: as she worked towards the completion of what would become *If I Don't Know*, she told an interviewer, 'All writers have blind spots, and I'm now very interested in locating my own.'[2] If her first two books were rooted in dissatisfactions, the second more bitterly than the first, *If I Don't Know* is rooted in satisfaction. It is also less consistently funny, much of the excoriating wit replaced with quiet and occasionally minimalist meditations on contentedness and its attendant sadnesses.

Serious Concerns contained its fair share of seriousness, intensity, and, ultimately, love, then; but it is in her third book that the realisation of the latter becomes a leitmotif. As Christina Patterson notes, 'Although you shouldn't conflate the "I" of a poem with the poet, you'd have to be a determined deconstructionist to ignore the fact that this was the first collection she wrote since finding love.'[3] Cope started living with the poet and critic Lachlan Mackinnon in 1994, two years after the publication of *Serious Concerns*, and Mackinnon (or 'LM') is the dedicatee of the volume and the apparent inspiration for many of its poems. It is, overwhelmingly, a more contented book, its moods less changeable; but, in part because it is not laced with parodies like *Making Cocoa for*

Kingsley Amis, nor full of despair spiced with angry wit like so much of *Serious Concerns*, several critics immediately pined for a return to the 'Wendy Cope' poems: Kate Kellaway, for example, reviewing the collection *in The Guardian*, suggested that 'something has been lost' from the earlier work, and considered that the 'safe mooring' of a steady life, to which Cope alludes in the poem 'Being Boring', 'is not always safe for her poems'.[4] Essentially, such commentators wanted more of the funny poems on which her reputation had rested and fewer successors to the less humorous poems she had always written and that had largely gone ignored; but, I would argue, they failed to appreciate the ways in which she has expanded her themes, and the often ingenious subtleties of her newer work. This chapter will address those.

The two Christmas-themed poems near the start of the book typify something of this change in tone and focus. Cope had included three Christmas poems in *Serious Concerns*, including the laconic and biting 'Another Christmas Poem', with its comically churlish cry 'bloody Christmas, here again', and advice to make men 'do the washing up' (*SC* 74). In *If I Don't Know*, we find 'The Christmas Life', which urges us instead to 'Bring in your memories of Christmas past. / Bring in your tears for all that you have lost' (*IIDK* 4). Here, Christmas is a time to take stock, as emphasised in the solemn, abrupt end-stopping of the lines and that laconic slant rhyme; it is not just something to have done with. We should notice the moment as it occurs. Facing that poem is '30th December', a poem of post-Christmas peace and year-end contemplation, in which 'everything is calm / And beautiful as the end of a hangover' (*IIDK* 5). There is both sadness and the peace of a loved routine in these two poems, and it might not be a stretch to read '30th December' as a metaphor for sudden calm in other contexts. The euphoric rush of being suddenly out of a hangover is, after all, simply the body returning to normal. There is contentment here, yes, but it is tinged by regret that the time left for contentment is inevitably shortening.

Of course, sadness about the inevitable isn't the same thing as misery at a predicament, which was behind many of the poems in her second collection. Cope has admitted that 'Misery creates more good poems',[5] and certainly her writing has slowed down since *Serious Concerns*: nine years separate that collection from *If I Don't Know*, and a full decade stands between that and her fourth, *Family Values*. The book lacks the scurrilous fire of her first collections, but it is also more thematically varied. And, for all its relative contentment, many of the poems are also invigorated by a tension between satisfaction and the anxiety that comes from knowing such moments must, ultimately, be transient. The opening poem, 'By the Round Pond', is a case in point, and sets the tone. The poem is an ekphrasis in response to Peter Rodulfo's painting *Lily Pool*, which shows a girl in an enchanting walled garden, staring into a lily-filled, wood-rimmed pond on a moonlit night that also seems to be daytime (there is a dragonfly in flight, for instance), with ethereal figures that might be statues in the wall behind. This short poem ends:

> You sit quite still and wonder when you'll go.
> It could be now. Or now. Or now. You stay.
> Who's making up the plot? You'll never know.
> Minute after minute swims away. (*IIDK* 3)

This is startlingly ambiguous: the first two quoted lines could simply refer to getting up and walking off, but also hint at the anxieties moments of solitude can leave us with, concomitant with the conscious awareness of time passing. The title poem, in which it is the speaker who sits in a moonlit garden in bloom, is a counterpart:

> I sit on the swing and cry.
>
> The rose. The gardenful. The evening light.
> It's nine o'clock and I can still see everything. (*IIDK* 6)

That last word seems also to encompass what is not physically present, and an agnostic's uncertainty that everything beautiful won't, one day, be taken.

In many respects, *If I Don't Know* in fact picks up where the penultimate section of *Serious Concerns* had left off, with what seemed there a new-found contentment in love, now deepened. The aforementioned 'Being Boring' admits that 'There was drama enough in my turbulent past'; now, 'If nothing much happens, I'm thankful':

> Someone to stay home with was all my desire
> And, now that I've found a safe mooring,
> I've just one ambition in life: I aspire
> To go on and on being boring. (*IIDK* 9)

This hints at the pained and generally thwarted desires repeated in many poems in *Serious Concerns*. However, the speaker is also aware that, ultimately, the survival of this condition is not entirely in her hands. Its continuation is an aspiration. Certainly, no state of life can ultimately be permanent. As the next poem in the book, a haiku forming the first part of her two 'Fireworks Poems', acknowledges:

> Faster and faster,
> They vanish into darkness:
> Our years together. (*IIDK* 10)

This phenomenon is supported by scientific research, which shows that, as people age, 'brain cells that produce the chemical messenger dopamine begin to deteriorate in the basal ganglia and substantia nigra, brain regions known to be involved in the internal clock':[6] cruelly, life seems to speed up as we near its end. As the poem's subtitle note tells us, it was intended as a performance piece of sorts, commissioned to be displayed in fireworks; the darkness following its transient intended existence in vivid colour is a crisp metaphor for the life we do have. It won't last, and we had better notice its highlights at the time.

'On a Train' symbolises the contentment of 'Being Boring', showing what that poem had told. The speaker gazes out at the shifting scene of 'fields, little lakes' and 'car park[s]' (*IIDK* 14). It is not, ostensibly, an especially unusual or 'beautiful' scene, although that is the adjective she uses for it, which speaks more to how experience shapes our perceptions of the world than to how they are objectively. Henry King correctly asserts that the poem is 'light in texture', but suggests it is demonstrative of 'her breadth of appeal com[ing] at a certain cost in depth'.[7] I would contest that he has missed the subtle implications of the poem's close, with its sudden wistful and alarmed, Housmanesque note: 'your hand in my hand, / still warm, still warm.' To notice this warmth as remarkable, and to repeat it, is to draw our attention, tacitly yet emphatically, to the possibility of its opposite. The title of the collection is a driving motivation, here and regularly throughout the book, for ultimately every positive emotion leaves the speaker wondering and not knowing what might happen to change it.

This mood of contentment tempered and invigorated by temporal anxiety and uncertainty returns in 'Tulips', written in the urgent, forceful, stop–start form of strict Sapphic stanzas:

> Every day I wonder how long they'll be here.
> Sad and fearing sadness as I admire them,
> Knowing I must lose them, I almost wish them
> Gone by tomorrow. (*IIDK* 52)

Tulips flower annually, so being 'sad and fearing sadness' at their inevitable departure seems, on the face of things, disproportionate. But, as is the case for comparable previously discussed lines near the ends of 'By the Round Pond' and 'If I Don't' Know', 'I must lose them' is ambiguous: does it mean the tulips dying down for the season, or the speaker one day not being there to see them, and measuring her life in seasonal cycles? The answer has to be both, and the shorter last line, taken on its own, has a powerful urgency, divorced from the 'almost wish' over a line break, manipulated into a stark and hopeless aphorism.

'Elegy for the Northern Wey' is another poem about abundance, treasuring it, and losing it, albeit in a more public context. In earlier poems, such as 'A Green Song' and 'The Concerned Adolescent', Cope had made a mockery of those fashionably jumping on environmentalist bandwagons in order to gain credit in a prestige economy (*SC* 20 and 21); this poem is an uncertain, sincere counterpart. In 1999, waste ammonia from a decommissioned ice cream factory polluted a thirteen-mile stretch of the northern branch of the River Wey in Hampshire, devastating much of the river's ecosystem.[8] The poem contains no human presences, as though to imply the river might be better off without us, and links four haiku stanzas, a form rooted in evocations of natural balance and the 'moment', a word repeated in the first and final stanzas. It presents a harmonious instant on a river 'busy with life', 'everything stirring' with the promise of new abundance at the start of spring, at a time 'we can never get back to' (*IIDK* 51).[9] But the poem then ends by contradicting this sober proclamation with another sudden observation: 'Look, a little frog'. Symbolically, this creature is solitary and vulnerable, but also new, young life. So, this 'elegy' is also a poem of hope, intimating a return to order both formally and, in its last line, explicitly.

This is a rather different approach to natural despoliation than those two witty poems in *Serious Concerns*, where the focus is on those keen to congratulate themselves for mitigating despoliation rather than on despoliation itself. This is somewhat indicative of how *If I Don't Know* is, on the whole, less humorous than its two predecessors, although the extent to which she has become a less witty poet has been overstated. There are certainly fewer bitter poems here, but her desire to lampoon egotism or inadvertent silliness had not evaporated. For example, 'A Hampshire Disaster' ridicules the clunkily passive voice adopted by so many local newspaper reporters: 'Shock was the emotion of most', and 'the courage and skill of the firefighters / was another emotion felt' (*IIDK* 42). (At least 'shock' is an emotion; 'courage and skill' are not.)

'A Poem on the Theme of Humour' highlights the perceived stupidity of prejudices against humorous poetry, and how inimical those prejudices are to the public perception of the art. Dedicated to Gavin Ewart, a poet who, like Cope, achieved considerable success while managing to be funny as well as serious, it begins with an epigraph from the rules of the 1994 Bard of the Year competition: 'Poems can be in any style and on any theme (except humour)' (*IIDK* 43). Even those parentheses demean humour, as though to suggest that it isn't really a style or theme in any case (and of course, strictly speaking, it isn't: this rule-maker has trouble with definitions comparable to the parodied newspaper hack in 'A Hampshire Disaster'). The poem takes an epistolary form, apparently championing the proclivities of the organisers while simultaneously highlighting how pointlessly wounding for the art it is: 'if humour is allowed into a poem, / People may laugh and enjoy it, / Which gives the poet an unfair advantage.' It is not Cope's wittiest poem, partly because it takes a loose and baggy free-verse form rather than crisply using one of the metrical forms she typically turns to that purpose, but it does make its point.

In the earlier poem 'Triolet', Cope described poets as 'mostly wicked as a ginless tonic' (*MC* 12). However, she has also observed that 'you don't often meet a poet who doesn't have a sense of humour, and some of them do keep it out of their poems because they're afraid of being seen as light versifiers. [...] It's all so high-minded.'[10] One such 'high-minded' but disappointing poet is the subject of 'A Reading', which follows 'A Poem on the Theme of Humour'; he might be the winner of such a contest:

> Everybody in the room is bored,
>
> Except the poet. We are his reward,
> Pretending to indulge his every quirk. (*IIDK* 45)

Note the interstanzaic enjambment, symbolically putting the poet in his own world, separate from everybody else 'in the room'. The poem is a villanelle, its shuffled repetitions echoing the boredom of the described event, its brevity pointedly not doing so. Cope has described poetry readings as 'a form of torture'[11] and 'the worst form of entertainment that has ever been invented',[12] and here the dullness is compounded by the subject's narcissism. Although her erstwhile poetic alter-ego Jake (or Jason) Strugnell has not reappeared since her first two collections, this lack of awareness and talent is straight out of the Strugnell playbook.

We are not given the identity of this poet, although any frequenter of poetry readings could name plenty of contenders. However, for the first time since *Making Cocoa for Kingley Amis,* in *If I Don't Know,* Cope does include several poems linked specifically to other writers and artists. In the Shakespearean sonnet 'The Sitter', a different kind of captive audience gets its – or her – own back. The poem is an ekphrasis in which the subject of an unflattering portrait, Vanessa Bell's *Nude* (*c.*1922–3), responds, through the explicatory medium of the written word. The poem was commissioned for the anthology *Writing on the Wall: Women Writers on Women Artists,*[13] and it is typical of Cope's mischievous desire not quite to do what she is told that she would respond to the job of celebrating a female artist by giving the anonymous (female) subject of a painting a voice against its creator. As the speaker points out, not only is she 'fat' in the portrait, her sunken body and downturned face and mouth make her seem 'Depressed and disagreeable' and 'ashamed' (*IIDK* 20). This poem has more than form in common with Shakespeare's 'Sonnet 18',[14] for like the subject of Shakespeare's poem she 'lives on' only in another's image, the friends who viewed her more flatteringly now 'all gone'. The poem playfully sees this unknown woman as the victim of the 'Admired, well-bred, artistic' Bloomsbury Group painter, and as such raises serious questions about who gets to control the narratives around the ways people lived and live, and the ways one class represents another.

Shortly after 'The Sitter', we find two poems of drily dispirited *ars poetica* facing each other, beginning a run of five self-reflexive poems about writing. 'Dead Sheep Poem' presents a contrast. In the morning, sheepskin rugs are seen for sale outside a village craft shop. Later, 'on the hillside', is another, 'creamy-white among the thistles', scrounging animals having 'cleared off long ago' – much as the potential purchaser of rugs has departed the shopfront (*IIDK* 22). And there, suddenly on the scene at the end of the poem, is the poet: 'The person with the notebook has arrived'. For the retailer (and customers), the pelts served a function. For the 'crows and maggots' who picked off the corpse on the hillside, the body did. The poet only turns up after, and we are further encouraged to consider the relationship between the poem's narrative and the art – the implication that the poet is another scavenger, but without a practical purpose – by the inclusion of the word 'Poem' in the title, unique in this collection.[15] This poem therefore has something in common with 'The Sitter', in that it portrays an artist taking advantage, although here that artist is the speaker.

Facing this poem is 'The Lyric Poet', an intertextual piece borrowing its form from Edwin Morgan's *Emergent Poems*, in which a line at the bottom of the poem is mined in columns above to produce different words,[16] and using a title and first line from Heinrich Heine: 'Ich mache die kleinen Lieder' ('I produce [the] little songs').[17] In that poem, a self-parody of sorts, Heine considers his former lover, her husband snoring beside her, and the children they have made together, and suggests that he would rather have the little babies than the little songs; it is an intriguing and perhaps telling choice of line for a childless poet in her fifties to borrow. Her poem turns Heine's on its head to some extent, presenting the poet as the 'child', who 'makes' poetry in desperate response:

a
ch i l   d
in
ne   ed
I ma   k e
a   l ine (*IIDK* 23)

Commentators keen to stress the apparently cosy satisfaction of Cope's work after *Serious Concerns* have not been quick to pick up on the implications of such poems. On the next page, 'A Mystery' presents a life of doing apparently very little apart from wanting to write such 'kleinen Leider', and occasionally doing so. The ending makes it almost a secondary title poem, and its feeling of uncertainty is a leitmotif of the collection: 'tomorrow someone will ask me, "What are you up to these days, what are you working on?" / And I still won't know' (*IIDK* 24).

A lyric poet likely has a different writing process to a novelist or screenwriter: she doesn't necessarily have a poem on the go, and must instead act on infrequent impulses. In 'The Squirrel and the Crow', set in a writing retreat and its environs, the enforced daily routine of 'Find notebook, summon muse' leads only to taking solace in the maxim *'Reading books is work'* – the sudden italics suggesting these words aren't her own and she might not believe them – and then to abandoning reading in favour of a walk (which evidently does, in fact, yield a poem) (*IIDK* 26). 'Reading Berryman's *Dream Songs* at the Writer's Retreat' presents the speaker in the same place, where she is expected to do what, for many poets, does not seem natural, and work continuously on the poems she hasn't yet been inspired to write.

The retreat in question – explicitly here, and implicitly in 'The Squirrel and the Crow' – is Hawthornden Castle in Scotland, a country house on a secluded estate, which offers month-long fellowships for writers and maintains a policy of silence between breakfast and evening.[18] Unsurprisingly, the poem takes the form of one of Berryman's poems in *The Dream Songs*: three six-line stanzas of apparent autobiography, complete with an interrogating friend who refers to her as 'Bones', and a Berrymanesque penchant for cramming lines with details (*IIDK* 25). Uniquely in this book, it owes something to the spirit of the parodies in her debut, presenting a bathetic counterpart to another poet's work. Here, most of the poem is concerned with the 'dreadful' experience of swimming in nearby public baths at the same time as unruly schoolchildren, which implies it is daytime and so she is bunking off her duties – like an unruly schoolchild. Moreover, her title offhandedly truncates Berryman's (*The Dream Songs*), with a similar insouciance to the way she treated Eliot's *The Waste Land* in the title of 'Waste Land Limericks' (*MC* 10).[19] But her poem is as unsettling as it is apparently silly:

> Once more to Hawthornden through Scottish fog.
> Back up to poet's lair and sit on bed.
> Is you bored, Bones, all by youzeself
> Wif read and write and bein' deep?
> Not for a moment.
> Now, a little sleep.

The penultimate line can be taken to mean two very different things: she hadn't been bored at all, and she hadn't been bored for a short time. Is she happy, after the swimming experience, to be alone with her thoughts? Maybe, but then as this is the point at which the otherwise unseen interlocutor, a metaphor for her private thoughts, has room to interrogate, and refers to her as 'Bones' with all of that epithet's intimations of mortality, we can't be sure. Certainly, though, the tacit obligation to be 'deep' at the retreat is at odds with the ostensible tone of the poem – much as the poem is also documentary evidence of poetry resulting from having been there.

In fact, the four poems she included from her month at Hawthornden Castle is a considerable haul, not least considering that the entire collection is the product of almost a decade.[20] Cope has attributed the time lapse between her second and third collections not only to increased happiness in her private life, but also to 'the battering I've taken off other poets. [...] It makes you think, "Well, perhaps I'm not any good", and, of course, that slows you down.'[21] 'The Ted Williams Villanelle' is a reminder, using the repetends of that tricky form both to enforce its point but also as a demonstration of skill, to 'do your thing', and ignore the 'sneers' of 'envious bastards' (*IIDK* 35). The poem takes its epigraph from the eponymous baseball star Ted Williams, 'Don't let anybody mess with your swing', and thereby implies that success in any field is at least in part the result of ignoring naysayers. It is dedicated to Ari Badaines, a clinical psychologist specialising in Gestalt therapy: an approach centred on helping clients to focus on the present moment rather than negative perceptions based on prior experience, and to prevent such negative thought patterns from clouding judgement. The poem, then, seems both a reminder to herself and a statement of intent, and also a deferential nod to the encouragement of others.

One figure who needs considerable encouragement is the character at the centre of 'The Teacher's Tale', which comprises part II of the collection, and runs to 678 lines of pentameter couplets, making it easily Cope's longest poem with the exception of *The River Girl*.[22] Framed in the past tense, like Chaucer's *Canterbury Tales*, it tells the story from early childhood to adolescence of Paul Skinner, a boy of socially conservative parents in 'London SE5' (*IIDK* 55), the postal district containing Camberwell, south London. There is little doubt that much of Cope's experience is projected into the poem, both in the unhappy child with a controlling mother (in an unpublished prose piece called 'A Misery Memoir', she makes this explicit),[23] and in what is probably the poem's most inspiring adult figure, his female primary school teacher: Cope had been one until the late 1980s, in the same area.

Paul, we learn, 'was not neglected / Or dressed in dirty clothes or underfed' (*IIDK* 57), but suffered malnourishment of another kind. His father was a weak man looking for an easy life, and his mother a domineering matriarch who wanted her child to grow up in her own snobby, emotionally stifled image:

> With attitudes and firm opinions this strict,
> They frowned upon most people in the district.
> And, naturally, they didn't want their boy
> To grow up like the local *hoi polloi*. (*IIDK* 55)

But is it 'natural' not to want your child to make friends in the neighbourhood? This is a brief moment of free indirect style, giving an insight into a mindset we are not encouraged to share. SE5 is a district of very mixed levels of social advantage, with Georgian villas and modern tower blocks of council-built housing, such as those of the (since-demolished) Elmington Estate, and between the large and more concentratedly working-class and racially diverse suburbs of Brixton and Peckham. *'Hoi polloi'* is obviously used with irony, but the modern pejorative use of the phrase – which in fact simply means 'the people' – has its origins in a nineteenth-century belief that refinement required knowledge of classical languages: it is a snob's term of address. Paul's parents were lower middle-class tradespeople, whose business relied on serving the very people they denigrated. And as the 'hoi polloi' in their area are mainly working class and often not white, they were not only classist, but also probably racist. Their misguided protection of their son was a manifestation of their own harmful prejudices, and could only be damaging in turn.

Paul Skinner is a counterpart to the eponymous hero of Charles Causley's famous poem 'Timothy Winters', but one with subtler problems. Both boys must rely on others and are failed, but Timothy Winters, who 'licks the patterns off his plate' at school lunchtime, is neglected materially and emotionally at home, and then also ignored at school and by the state.[24] Paul, by contrast, was ostensibly every bit the cared-for child, and it took a percipient teacher to notice the problem. This is crucial, and ultimately might have made all the difference. That teacher, Mrs Moore, found 'the little lad / Was often serious, subdued and sad', and realised that the parents 'might well be / The cause of his unhappiness' (*IIDK* 58). Then, at the end of his final year at primary school, another teacher, Mr Browning, took Paul aside and told him to remember that he was 'bright' and 'likeable', even though 'Your life is sometimes difficult, I know' (*IIDK* 63). Again, the book's title is relevant here: we might ask what difference it makes – emotionally, if not materially – that the teachers *did* know.

All the same, at secondary school, he fell into the wrong company, finding popularity by learning to 'play the fool': 'He might as well, since nothing but perfection / Would win him mum's approval and affection' (*IIDK* 68). Paul's mother has indeed always expected nothing less than 'perfection', but perfection is almost always an illusory ideal. Moreover, to her, perfection entails perfect obedience, and children learn by finding their own way as much as by following rules set out for them. The poem closes with him in his mid-teenage years, not quite coming of age, finally learning to express his emotions, and having insights beyond his domineering mother's control: 'If only [his dad] had had a different wife' (*IIDK* 75). He leaves home at sixteen, survives 'tough' bedsit years, passes his A levels, and gets to college. And here we are reminded of the importance of those earlier teachers, who had understood: 'when he felt depressed and all alone / The thought of all the people he had known / Who'd liked him kept him going' (*IIDK* 76). The poem ends with a sort of coda, shifting into the present tense to sketch his current circumstances after the poem's detailed portrait of his past: 'He teaches nowadays', and is especially good with 'troubled children who have been oppressed / At home' (*IIDK* 76).

Paul Skinner is not Wendy Cope, of course, but there are distinct parallels: both became teachers; both 'see a shrink' in young adulthood and find it 'help[s]'; and both had ostensibly comfortable middle-class childhoods but experienced a repressive home life with apparently domineering mothers, a circumstance she explores in her next collection. The poem can be seen as an allegory for her lived experience, filtered through fiction: it is, explicitly, a 'tale', and Paul a 'character'. *Family Values* would engage with the subject more personally.

4

'Your anger is a sin': *Family Values* (2011)

Wendy Cope went into psychoanalysis in the early 1970s, shortly after the death of her father. As she said in 2011, the year her fourth collection *Family Values* was published,

> I got in touch with all sorts of powerful feelings that I didn't know I had. I needed to do something with them, and writing poems turned out to be helpful. I think I had been very oppressed by my mother and it was something to do with just creating a space where I was free, inside my own head – and then extending this space on to a piece of paper.[1]

However, as we have seen, most of her earliest published poems were not especially personal or revealing. This changed with her second and third collections, where the primary ostensibly personal focus is on finding a committed romantic relationship and experiencing one, respectively. As Andrew Motion puts it, there has been 'a gradual move towards the candidly autobiographical' in her poetry (Lewis), although this rarely turned to childhood in those three books. *If I Don't Know* ends with 'The Teacher's Tale', a coming-of-age narrative about a boy's difficult home life (*IIDK* 55–76). *Family Values*, in which she focuses on aspects of her own childhood with a religious and controlling mother, makes that poem seem a paralogue for her own experiences, and was her first collection to appear after her mother's death – a circumstance she says helped her not to 'put poems [she wrote about her mother] aside'.[2] The collection also finds her wrestling for the first time with the possibility of Christian faith, before ultimately seeming to reject it. This book therefore expands her range of subjects, the tension at its heart being her own past and the moral codes that underpinned it.

The title reeks of irony, the phrase 'family values' redolent of American right-wing rhetoric about the importance of the God-fearing nuclear family. However, the book has little of the anger or febrility of *Serious Concerns*; rather, it is often as contemplatively wistful as *If I Don't Know*, if also more frequently unsettled. Her first two collections begin with something comical and socially pointed ('Engineers' Corner' in *Making Cocoa for Kingsley Amis*, 'Bloody Men' in *Serious Concerns*); her third opens with calmly anxious *memento mori* ('By the Round Pond'). This is emblematic of the books themselves: the third is calmer, and rages against less, except the potential dying of the light. *Family Values* begins with 'A Christmas Song', which is similarly contemplative, but which extends back out to wider public concerns. It begins by asking why Christ would cry in the manger. The obvious answer is that he cries because babies do so, as a prelinguistic way of communicating need. However, Christ, we are told, died for our sins, and lived for our salvation, and so it makes sense that he cries 'for the people / Who greet this day with dread': because 'somebody dear' to them is dead, their 'love affairs went wrong', or they are 'separated parents' grieving 'While children hang their stockings up / Elsewhere on Christmas Eve' (*FV* 3). The poem juxtaposes the Christian *raison d'être* of Christmas, and what it has become: the clichéd 'season of good cheer', the only time of year when almost everyone is culturally pressured into seeming happy, which is not the same as feeling it. This tension is the leitmotif of Cope's many Christmas poems: Christmas is a time for merriment, but we are not machines who can turn on the appropriate feelings.[3] This poem is the apotheosis of that sentiment in her work, and by invoking Christ's suffering for humanity, she implies that such culturally enforced 'good cheer' is, in fact, deeply unchristian.

Cope was raised by an Evangelical mother and sent at seven to an Anglican boarding school, but grew to reject Christianity. Her atheism then thawed in middle age – first towards belief, although she now professes herself to be 'agnostic' (*Desert Island Discs*). In 2001, referring to an incident in 1995, she said that until that point 'all my published work had been written at a time when I thought of myself as an atheist', but that in that year she 'had begun going to church again after a gap of more than thirty years', and had started to 'explore [the] possibilities [of God]' – an explicitly non-atheist position.[4] From the late 1990s, she started regularly to attend evensong at Winchester Cathedral, and 'was so moved by it I tried to persuade myself that I believed it all. I almost succeeded.'[5] 'A Christmas Song' begins a run of four poems about Christmas at the beginning of the collection, in which that 'almost'-Christian sensibility – something not otherwise much in evidence in her poetry – slowly modulates into a culturally Christian one. That is intriguing in a collection that later explores explicitly atheistic or agnostic notions (as we shall see): *Family Values* begins by making the case for Christian worship, before arguing its way back to agnosticism. The second poem, 'Christmas Ornaments', is a personalised counterpart to the first, in the sense that it expresses gratitude for having 'someone to come home to', who can 'share' her satisfaction at having collected trinkets over the years, symbols of love deepening with time (*FV* 4). But it also makes clear that this couple display 'the Holy Family' at Christmas, and collect ornaments from churches, both of which reveal a culturally Christian sensibility beyond the secular norm, if not necessarily an avowedly religious one. In the next two poems, 'Cathedral Carol Service' and 'O Come, All Ye Faithful', the speaker immerses, and remembers being immersed, in Christian ceremony. The latter remembers her father who, we are told, would always fastidiously change 'citizens' to 'denizens' in the eponymous hymn, because Heaven is 'not a city'; now, she does the same, in tribute (*FV* 6). This makes the last two lines, in which she is 'singing, rather quietly, / "Denizens of Heaven above"', an imperative plea (the full line is 'Sing all ye citizens [or denizens] of heaven above'), addressed to her father and to his supposed afterlife in a place she cannot visit and that the poem has not quite confessed she believes in.

This begins the collection's turn to poems focused on family matters. 'Differences of Opinion', in two parts, repeats from *If I Don't Know* a short poem in rhyming couplets, called 'He Tells Her' (*IIDK* 36), about a man in a relationship assuming he is right when he isn't – the sort of poem we might more readily associate with *Serious Concerns*.[6] However, here this is paired with a longer poem in which a mother does much the same with a child, and in which we see religion being used as a stick, rather than being something we choose to engage with on our own terms. This second part, 'Your Mother Knows', shows a woman being as stupid as some men can be: 'Your mother knows the earth's a plane / And, challenged, sheds a martyr's tear' (*FV* 7). The mother is in a position of parental dominance, assumes she knows best, clearly doesn't, and expects automatic compliance from her offspring – like the mother in 'The Teacher's Tale'.

'Your Mother Knows' is in seven tetrameter quatrains of interlocking rhyme, and is a pantoum, a form that repeats the second and fourth lines of each stanza as the first and third of the next. As with many of Cope's other poems in repeating forms, such as the villanelles 'Lonely Hearts' (*MC* 17) and 'A Reading' (*IIDK* 45), the repetends are used to suggest a grinding circularity to proceedings. The speaker is in a conundrum: she cannot agree with the mother because 'It's very bad to tell a lie. / All this has been ordained by God', so 'It's hard to see what you can do'. Moreover, by putting the poem in the second person, she forces some of that conundrum on the reader:[7]

> You're difficult. You don't fit in.
> God gave her strength to bear this pain.
> You know your anger is a sin.

The second sentence in the first of these lines might in part be the product of experience, but the first two words sound like the internalised comment of the parent, and otherwise this feels like received parental 'wisdom' filtered through a version of Christian faith. This immediately complicates the responses to Christianity in the early part of the book, which demonstrated a fondness for religious ritual. If we consider the collection as its own 'poem', its constituent parts presented in the order the poet intends them to be read, it is as though Cope is interrupting the Christianised sentiments at the beginning with a reminder of the pernicious purposes the same doctrines had been put to earlier in her life.

The poem makes us want to reverse its one-way communication and reach inside, to tell the speaker she is not wrong for being right. It is possible to read it as a clear metaphor for other situations in which a domineering parent might wish to enforce her worldview, and use Christian concepts of parental duty for that purpose.[8] The next poem, 'Sunday Morning', presents a situation not unlike 'Your Mother Knows' in its logical impossibility, but this time in the first person:

> Will I go along
> To church with Mummy or stay home,
> Depressed and in the wrong?
>
> It's a communion service
> And I cannot go up,
> A doubter and a sinner,
> To take the silver cup. (*FV* 9)

The mother decides 'angrily' that it is better the child stay home, so as not to shame them both, 'Which means another ruined day / For Mummy and for me'. That is the end of both the poem and the matter, and it is hard to know what the child could have done to improve the situation other than comply fully with her mother's moral code and not reach her own existential conclusions.

'You're Not Allowed' is another thematic counterpart to 'Your Mother Knows', this time to the extent that both poems share a metrical pattern (and a homophone) in their titles, and both are extended pantoums in which the repeated lines overemphasise the illogical conclusions. It is about being sent to boarding school at seven. The child is evidently emotionally trapped by the dominant parent, and again apparently slips in and out of parroting what seem to be the parent's phrases. The poem is consistently in lines of strict iambic pentameter, which means that when the last repeating line comes, 'Things *will* get better, if you're very good' (my emphasis), we are encouraged to place an awkward stress on the very word the child is most likely to doubt (*FV* 10). 'Boarders' then reflects on the effects of that schooling, and each of its reflections is qualified and uncertain. It is not a happy poem, but it does imply human growth, albeit in a scenario where overbearing parental control has to some extent been replaced by overbearing peer pressure. The speaker was teased ('our word for bullying') for using 'too many long words' (*FV* 15), but did this serve as a valuable lesson? 'I soon learned not to. / Look at how I write', she concludes, those two monosyllabic lines of simple sentences serving as an emphatic answer, underwritten by the book's preceding twelve pages.

While these poems are close to being relentless in their explicit or implicit criticism of the mother, they are also calm. Being angry about 'Bloody men' made sense in *Serious Concerns*, because those poems spoke about a circumstance that was ostensibly ongoing; but these are phlegmatic poems of memory, the events long gone, the possibilities of change gone with them. 'Brahms Cradle Song', the most phlegmatic of them all, is the closest thing in the book to a poem of reconciliation, and coolly lists the positives: she 'read me *Black Beauty*' (but only that one book?), 'made me learn the piano' (although even here the first verb belies an unwelcome authoritarianism), and 'taught me to swim' and 'to drive', and

> For all that, I am grateful.
> As for the rest, I can begin
> To imagine forgiving her [...]. (*FV* 21)

This 'all' amounts to four things, and is presented as exhaustive. It is a paltry list, in the scheme of things. The stiff formality of the phrasing echoes the stiff formality of the parent with whom we have been presented in the preceding poems; and, crucially, to 'begin / To imagine forgiving' means that has not happened yet. Besides, it is too late now anyway, at least interpersonally. As she notes in 'Greydawn', 'I have spun through the air / Into the future, all by myself' (*FV* 22).

'Sunday Morning' implies that, as a child, the speaker had decided she did not believe in God (she is 'a doubter') and had failed to observe at least her mother's notion of a Christian code of conduct (she is also 'a sinner'). 'Keep Saying This', in the middle of the collection and shortly after its poems about Christian ritual and upbringing, contemplates the other end of life, implies a constancy of faithlessness, and encourages us to use the finite nature of existence as a spur – which led her partner, the poet Lachlan Mackinnon, to write 'anti-Larkin' on a copy of the typescript.[9] This poem is a villanelle, so another poem in a repeating form, although here the repetends constitute a mantra. Villanelles repeat two rhymed lines four times each in their nineteen lines, and then bring them together as a final couplet. This one ends:

No point in living if you let
Your terror of the end take hold.
Keep saying this and don't forget
The party isn't over yet. (*FV* 27)

A colon at the end of the penultimate line might have helped, because this is a reminder not to give in to the fear of death – but it does not deny that there *is* 'terror' implicit in the notion that this metaphorical 'party' is not eternal, nor that death *will* be 'the end'. The next poem, 'Once I'm Dead', reasons that 'I won't mind being dead', again using a repeating form (a triolet) to interrogate a circular thought (*FV* 28). If this is also a mantra, it becomes a less certain and more Larkinesque one very quickly, because 'still I dread / The day that we must part, myself and I'. The phrasing even echoes Larkin's most painful poem about death, 'Aubade', which meditates on 'the dread / Of dying, and being dead', and the 'sure extinction that we travel to' (Larkin, 115–16). Kate Kellaway suggests that in 'Once I'm Dead' Cope is 'playful about her fear of extinction'.[10] Formally, this is certainly playful; but to pass it off as a witty ditty is unfairly and unfoundedly to typecast the poet. The poem is as serious as anything, its 'playful' formal circularity working as a downward spiral, echoing an interrogative thought from which there is no escape.

The collection's few subsequent poems alluding to matters of faith are also more atheistic than agnostic. 'April' is a reverdie, a genre thrilling to the arrival of spring, canonical examples of which in English include the thirteenth-century 'The Cuckoo Song', which begins 'Sumer is i-comen in— / Lhude sing cuccu!' ('Summer is coming in, / Loudly sing, cookoo!'),[11] and 'Home-Thoughts, From Abroad' by Robert Browning, whose celebration of England in April includes 'the chaffinch sing[ing] on the orchard bough' (*Norton Anthology of Poetry*, 1017). Both of these are echoed in Cope's opening lines, 'The birds are singing loudly overhead / As if to celebrate the April weather' (*FV* 34). The poem is more than simple evocation, though, for that is intensified by the same tension that, in her previous collection, had precipitated tears in the title poem (*IIDK* 6), or the piquant delight at finding her partner's hand 'still warm, still warm' in 'On a Train' (*IIDK* 14). In 'April', unlike in those poems, she is explicit about the underlying anxiety: 'I don't believe I'll see you when we're dead. / I don't believe we'll meet and be together.' These staccato sentences leave no room for ambiguity, and the first-person pronouns that start these and two more of the poem's eight lines proclaim the human experience of facing up to this existential angst with a calm dignity. Again, the subject is Larkinesque, but here she has regained a full, unLarkinesque composure in the face of it, echoed in the balancing, phlegmatic use of anaphora. This is the same dignity and control she displayed in the poems about her upbringing earlier in the book, and it shouldn't be mistaken for a lack of passion or gravity.

The same sentiment, and certainty, are central to 'At Steep', set near to the East Hampshire village where Edward Thomas, in 1914, wrote his first mature poetry, and where a memorial plaque to him is mounted on a rock on the Shoulder of Mutton Hill. The poem calls to mind Alun Lewis's 'To Edward Thomas': both are addressed to their predecessor, and set at his small memorial. Lewis compares himself to Thomas, largely unfavourably, and finds, as well as kinship, a sense that he is 'somehow apart, / lonely and exalted by the friendship of the wind'.[12] Cope is more explicit that Thomas will not hear her address, and is not looking down from an afterlife, but is 'beyond all company. / Numbers and words inscribed on stone / Are all that's left of you' – and of course they never were part of him in the first place (*FV* 37). Nonetheless, 'you're dead and gone and speaking still. / Your spirit lives'. This is the spirit in the poems, a poet's only hope of life beyond death, and one that does the poet no personal good: as Cope's poem has it, 'You cannot know, and never will'.

One of the book's best-known poems, 'Spared', a meditation on loneliness in company and an elegy for the victims of 9/11, puts all notions of faith to one side, but offers the humanist notion also emphasised by Christian doctrine that 'love' is paramount (*FV* 45). As Sophie Hannah notes, 'the emotion is all the more powerful for being restrained by the paired disciplines of cautious intelligence and traditional form'[13] (it is in quatrains of tetrameters with an interlocking rhyme scheme). There is also restraint in delicately framing the poem as a meditation on fortune, not misfortune. The title has religious connotations, implying a deity who chooses who lives and dies, but here the speaker and her addressee ('It wasn't you, it wasn't me'), are 'spared' only by an arbitrary quirk of fate that meant they were not in the wrong place at the wrong time, were not left to give 'A last farewell on the machine / While someone sleeps another hour', or to 'Send helpless love across the sky'. 'The sky' offers no help; we must rely on one another.

The book's last poem, 'Closedown', concerning the 'messages across the sky' of the shipping forecast, is about a far more quotidian kind of loneliness in company. Carol Ann Duffy, in her poem 'Prayer', refers to the shipping forecast as 'the radio's prayer':[14] it comes at the end of the day, to most of us it is largely inscrutable but it puts words to the elemental, and it represents a *de facto* collective and individual ritual. Many who hear it – often at night, on the radio – have no purpose for it, but it can be consoling nonetheless. In 'Closedown', Cope's speaker goes to the studio to hear and watch it being announced, and the dedicatee is the BBC shipping forecast announcer Alice Arnold. The poem does not refer to her, however, instead presenting an everywoman or everyman, 'Someone, all alone', who

> Speaks into the darkness,
> Says a last goodnight,
> Plays the national anthem,
> Switches off the light. (*FV* 66)

This is secular liturgy, a lonely reminder of collective loneliness, and as much a part of the routine, or tradition, as the subsequent playing of the national anthem. And, of course, by having a visitor on this occasion and potentially others, the announcer is symbolically not alone in this instance.

The sequence '*from* The Audience', also near the end of the book, turns much of that on its head, to depict isolation in company. Its eight sections present a melange of audience members at a classical concert, and the 'from' in the title implies that its characters are representative of the bigger picture. All no doubt appear to be having a good time to those around them, and none is, or at least not entirely. This is perfect subject matter for Cope's brand of mild social mockery, and she exploits it. However, the sequence also homes in on the individualism of the experiences by moving from the relative intimacy of a free indirect third person in the first two poems, to the first person, and from ultimately superficial and fleeting concerns, to poignant hope and vulnerability, to the consolations of reliving a vanquished past. 'The Cougher', holding it in, wishes he or she was 'Safe at home with a CD, / In an armchair, free to cough the whole way through' (*FV* 51);[15] 'The Traditionalist', given a perfectly traditional and regular triolet in which to speak, pines for 'the days before music went wrong' (*FV* 52), while 'The Radical' considers the concert 'post-modern, easy listening' and does not feel 'antagonised enough' (*FV* 53); the 'First Date' couple – each given a poem with the same title, reflecting the isolated similarity of their experiences – listen as attentively as they can manage in order to have something to say afterwards, and assume the other is 'totally lost in the music' (*FV* 55–6). The sequence is largely an exploitation of witty possibilities, then, but it is also a reminder that society comprises individuals, and that we cannot often tell what people are feeling. It then culminates by taking a more poignant turn, with 'The Widow', who uses her Shakespearean sonnet – a form traditionally used for poems of love-longing – to muse that this future has arrived 'so fast. / When we were young it seemed so far away' (*FV* 57). This recalls the 'far away' childhood evoked with apparent clarity much earlier in the book. Here, Cope has invented a character to provide a reminder to cherish what you have while you have it, and to stay at the 'party' until it is over, empathetic to the spirit of 'Keep Saying This', earlier in the book. That would become the dominant theme in her next, and most recent, collection.

5

'About the human heart': *Anecdotal Evidence* (2018)

With its frequent contemplations on ageing and memory, Wendy Cope's fifth collection has much in common with its predecessor, *Family Values*. However, here she is even more consistently introspective, and an even greater proportion of the poems are in the serious but conversational, unrhymed free verse she has always tended to use for such explorations. As the title implies, this collection is largely about taking stock, and the proof offered by memory for where we have come from. But it is also often a book about coming to terms with what we will never do.

This is exemplified by the epiphanic 'Orb', early in the collection, in which the 'illuminated orb' on a 'black background', with 'faint / red lines that could be rivers', is not, we discover, a planet viewed through a telescope, but 'my eyeball / on the optician's screen', part of a 'mysterious universe / I'll never explore' (*AE* 6). The speaker is eyeball to eyeball with the uncanny unfamiliarity of herself, an observer of her own scientific reality. We tend to think of the 'universe' in expansive terms, and of exploration as pushing farther, higher, deeper, to places we have not been. We do much of that exploring with eyes: they are so familiar, conceptually, as to seem mundane. This poem is a reminder to look inwards as well, and turns that literal looking into a metaphor, for 'We know so little of ourselves, / and of each other'. By so doing, we might not only learn about ourselves, but about our common humanity. This is a darkness we can 'scan / like astronomers' (note how the enjambment forces us to 'scan' the width of the poem as we read it), to recover and give meaning to our 'half-forgotten stories'.

If introspection allows us to remember our stories, poetry might allow us to immortalise and share them, but to what end? In the short opening poem, 'Evidence', Cope posits the age-old question, italicising it to indicate that it is not hers: *'What's the use of poetry?'* (*AE* 6). In draft, she had added *'or of any art'*, but this is dropped in the final version, limiting the question to her art form.[1] It is a question often answered by writers and philosophers, perhaps most famously Samuel Johnson, in his apothegmatic comment that 'the only end of writing is to enable readers better to enjoy life or better to endure it'.[2] Thomas Hardy, quoting his friend Leslie Stephen, noted a different function, empathy: 'The ultimate aim of the poet should be to touch our hearts by showing his own.'[3] It is to this way of thinking in particular that Cope subscribes, and in 'Evidence' she responds with her own dictum: poetry is, or can be, 'anecdotal evidence / About the human heart'.

Indeed, this collection is full of hearty anecdotes, and is often personal and revealing – perhaps more directly and conspicuously so than any of her others. Hardy, quoting Stephen, continued that a poet should not 'exhibit his learning, his fine taste, or his skill' (Hardy, 171). It is a view with which Cope's work has increasingly implied sympathy. Her first and second collections contained a number of literary jokes; the third, fourth, and fifth collections contained a number of poems responding to other poets or artists. These require at least some prior knowledge of their subject to be effective, but relatively little. But in *Anecdotal Evidence*, a higher proportion even than in *Family Values* elucidate apparently personal memories, and pair these with a sense of solitude in the company of ghosts. In the second poem, 'The Damage to the Piano', she writes, 'I am cast adrift / with all this furniture / and no-one to tell me off' (*AE* 4).[4] It is a near-repetition of the sentiment expressed at the end of 'Greydawn', in *Family Values*, in which she mentions three remaining plates from a set she'd used as a child, and then notes: 'I have spun through the air / Into the future, all by myself' (*FV* 22). The difference is that here she imagines the 'hell' that would 'break loose' if her mother were alive to see an heirloom damaged. This is a poem about the psychological scars that are inherited, not the goods. It is evidently good not to be lambasted, but that realisation lies outside the poem: in it, the thought leaves her feeling 'cast adrift'.

A comparable fear of isolation is at the heart of 'Bags', a poem about trying to re-inhabit a past life by beginning again to use the shoe and laundry bags 'embroidered / by Nanna: W. M. COPE' and once taken to boarding school (*AE* 9). In its final third, this poem shifts from subjective first person to objective third person, to describe the speaker's childhood self as a separate entity, vulnerable in a 'place / where she didn't know anyone / and nobody knew her name'. Reusing the bags is a wilful act of memorialisation, and precipitates a memory that is not wholly negative, because it is also a memory of love from 'the grandmother / who couldn't prevent her / from being sent away'.

This book's few poems about an often-difficult childhood obviously have counterparts in the greater number of such poems in *Family Values*. While Cope's themes and styles have shifted over time, as we have seen, she rarely exhausts a new theme in one book, and often the poems interrogating one set of circumstances spill into her subsequent collection, even if they then have a slightly different timbre – as with her Strugnell poems, for example, most of which are in *Making Cocoa for Kingsley Amis*, with a few more in *Serious Concerns*. Her poems about childhood in *Anecdotal Evidence* tend to end with at least some uplift, a gift from memory: in spite of everything, they imply, those experiences were worth having. Memories can bring back the difficult things we have experienced, but also can remind us that we overcame them. 'Upheavals', for example, about the end of a school holiday and the impending return to boarding school, begins with 'dread' but ends with a nascent, self-determined coming of age: back at school, 'I was all right. I wished / my parents would leave me alone' (*AE* 11).

The sonnet 'Reunion', on the other hand, is about the inability to relive past happiness, and the often-painful gulf between now and then, felt when we are forced to recognise it at close quarters. This poem evokes the joy and sorrow of collective memory at a class reunion, the speaker travelling both to another location and, in a sense, 'to the past' to find friends from her schooldays, nearly five decades on (*AE* 16).

However, the event precipitates doubt as well as joy: 'You are the same, it seems to me. Am I?' Of course, nobody is, although the uncanny experience encourages fanciful delusions, and the poem ends with a bump, marooned back in what it describes as the 'future, where I'm sad to know / It's over. It was over long ago.' Memory can be tantalising: the closer we get to reliving it, the more we are forced to stand face to face with inevitable, irreversible change.

This poem, and 'An Afternoon', which faces it, are Shakespearean sonnets, a form used for seventeen of the book's fifty-two poems. In both, she turns a theme traditionally reserved for poems of unrequited love to considerations of the one-way nature of memory. 'An Afternoon' uses the present tense to get inside what is recalled: the speaker is at university with her parents who are making a fly-by visit, and is 'depressed. I haven't said' (*AE* 17). The parents have been to a funeral nearby, and seek comfort from their daughter. Thematically, the turn of this sonnet comes not at the expected place, after the octave, but with the final four lines, which shift to the past tense and the present reality. The effect is that most of the poem is given over to evoking what happened, with only a short space being left for a terse, near-reconciliatory comment on that:

> I hope the hugs and smiles I gave them eased
> Their grief. Years later, when they're dead,
> I will remember and be moved to say
> I never loved them more than on that day.

The parents got 'hugs and smiles', although there is no indication they recognised their daughter was also struggling. The twelfth line delivers the first shock, though: they are dead now themselves, and cannot be turned to for reciprocation, and unless we place an awkward stress on 'Years', the line uniquely scans as a tetrameter, not a pentameter, formally echoing that something is now missing. The last line then provides a heart-breaking surprise: the young woman took what comfort she could.

Cope has not become a parent. However, in 2013 she married Lachlan Mackinnon, with whom she had lived since 1994, and that is the apparent subject of two adjacent poems, 'A Vow' and

'To My Husband' – poems that look forwards, rather than to the past. The former is the wedding poem of a pragmatist who 'cannot promise never to be angry' nor 'that I will deserve you' (*AE* 21). By contrast, the latter radiates *carpe diem* sentimentality, and is full of reminders, as Philip Larkin put it in 'The Mower', to 'be kind / While there is still time'.[5] This sonnet contains three rhymed couplets, a sestet's worth of 'couples' with two at its start and one at the end, and begins: 'If we were never going to die, I might / Not hug you quite as often or as tight' (*AE* 22). Here, death, and the shortening of time, is a motivator; while she admits she 'Would [...] want to change things, if I could', the fact that she cannot thwart death is instigation to 'value every day' of married life.

In the Shakespearean sonnet 'The Tree', which recalls 'Christmas Ornaments' (*FV* 4), memory is then joyously sewn to the present, embellishing it, rather than being divorced from the present as it had been in 'Reunion' and 'An Afternoon'. 'The Tree' expresses comfort in looking back and seeing an unbroken trail of breadcrumbs into an enriching past. The Christmas tree is 'hung with treasures', but ones of a sentimental not financial kind, for they are only 'little trinket[s]' and each 'tells a story, / A memoir of the life we had before' (*AE* 25). These serve as reminders that the couple have always 'got through the disruption and the pain' and, as such, they may also prove fortifying reminders in the future. This is a contented poem, inherently lacking the heightened tensions of her most emotive work; but this contentment relies on reminders that it cannot last forever.

In 2011, Cope and Mackinnon moved from the small cathedral city of Winchester to the smaller one of Ely, Cambridgeshire, following Mackinnon's retirement from Winchester College. Winchester is never explicitly mentioned in her poetry. Ely, by comparison, has uniquely and quickly inspired two paeans to a hometown, 'anecdotal evidence' of being somewhere that is a stay against the huge world beyond, at once apart from it and connected. Characteristically for Cope, when she wishes to present two takes on one subject or circumstance, these poems comprise one double-page spread. In the first, 'Here We Are',

Long goods trains trundle past.
Maersk, China Shipping,
China Shipping, Maersk.

Big world out there. (*AE* 26)

Those companies' names are familiar to anyone who has seen the sides of a fair share of goods trains in Britain, or in many other countries: they are global, but also represent Denmark and China, small and huge, Europe and the opposite side of the world, west and east, north and south, near and far. The final line – a simple, truncated, separated sentence – hardly needs saying, although it is worth noticing that 'out there' is not here, and symbolically the carriages are only passing through, one after another. That 'world' beyond offers the comfort of potential connection, but is also a reminder of the greater comfort in finding 'ourselves, / happy to sit beside the river' – another thoroughfare – 'and watch the trains go by'.

In that poem's counterpart, 'Ely', the speaker and her partner – 'We' – decide to reject the common theory that the city 'got its name / From eels', and that 'The Isle of Eels became / the Isle of Ely', in favour of 'A newer theory, out of academe' that the city is an ancient 'paradise': 'our new home / Is in a city called Elysium' (*AE* 27).[6] This draws on a draft poem about Ely Cope had abandoned, written in October 2011, shortly after their move, which begins 'When you're in Paradise / It's a good idea to notice',[7] the later, finished 'Ely' articulating this through possibly fanciful evidence. 'Ely' calls back to 'To My Husband', as if to say we are in our earthly, if temporal, heaven already. It is an unabashedly syrupy proclamation of a kind her younger self, the author of *Serious Concerns*, might have rejected, or found implausible. This is the apotheosis of contentment, as part of a couple, half of an 'our'.

Two other poems in the collection are about memory and the present in the context of a different man, the speaker's father, who had only been the partial focus of one poem in her previous collection's run of family poems. 'Baggage', about finding her father's 'battered suitcase', recalls as best it can his 'mysterious' travels, and ends with a desperate bid at reunion: 'The child of his old age, I close my eyes / And join him under sunny, foreign skies' (*AE* 5). That, of course, is a rhyming couplet in strict iambic pentameters, which is hardly unusual for this often metrical, formally adept poet. However, the poem also shows a new tendency in Cope's work, for elsewhere in the poem, the metre and especially the rhyme are initially quite loose, with three of the poem's previous rhymes being slant rhymes ('here' / 'where', 'long' / 'young', 'glamorous' / 'was'). The poem comes 'right', softly and triumphantly, at the final moment of heartbreakingly elusive togetherness.

Another poem about her father and permanence, 'My Father's Shakespeare', alludes to Shakespeare's 'Sonnet 18'.[8] When passing the eponymous volume down,

> He wrote, 'To Wendy Mary Cope. With love.'
> Love on a page, surviving death and time.
> He didn't even have to make it rhyme. (*AE* 36)

We might be reminded of Tony Harrison's 'Book Ends II', in which he acknowledges that he 'can't squeeze more love' into an inscription for his dead mother's gravestone than his father had managed in his 'mis-spelt, mawkish, stylistically appalling' attempt on scrap paper – while, like Cope, putting that comment into rhymed, metred verse, from which it derives part of its impact.[9] Cope's equivalent has finality and certainty granted to it by being a closing couplet.

In the middle of the book are two runs of several poems not placed under single headings, as sequences would be, but that are clearly interconnected both thematically and formally. The second contains the aforementioned poems regarding Shakespeare, which we shall come to shortly. The first, and shorter, turns Japanese syllabic forms to a quintessentially English setting, and (although this is not made explicit) seems to return to Ely and the River Great Ouse that flows past it, again implying the separateness and nonetheless global interconnectedness of that place. Cope had previously published several witty quips in haiku form, such as 'Strugnell's Haiku' (*MC* 54) and 'Haiku: Looking Out of the Back Bedroom Window without My Glasses' (*IIDK* 7).[10] By contrast, the three syllabic poems in *Anecdotal Evidence* are quiet reflections, the latter two in a form she had not previously used, and which is uncommon in English.

In the first, 'Haiku: Willows', frozen branches resemble fireworks that 'sparkled / and froze in the air' (*AE* 29). That last line is the only one of the three comprising monosyllabic words, as though to emphasise chaotic fire turning to solid, separated ice. Most English willows are weeping, and that provides the wrong image for fireworks, but Japanese pussy willows tend to reach up in scraggly lines, and there is nothing explicitly English about what the poem depicts. The next poem, 'Naga-Uta', is named for an expandable Japanese syllabic form meaning 'long poem', although Cope's is really an extended tanka, with two extra lines of, respectively, five and seven syllables before the final seven-syllable line. The poem formally hybridises traditions, beginning with four lines that distinctly recall the declarative and alliterative norms of Old English verse:

> Clearest of clear days:
> frozen leaves under my feet,
> frost on bare branches,
> blue sky, smoke from the funnel. (*AE* 30)

Unlike 'Haiku: Willows', the poem distinctly engages with a quintessentially English lowland scene, with 'a narrowboat' on 'the quiet river'. This links it to the third poem, 'By the River', a tanka, which maintains the more specific location of the second poem but transports us to the other side of the year:

> The day is so still
> you can almost hear the heat.
> You can almost hear
> that royal blue dragonfly
> landing on the old white boat. (*AE* 31)

This is a meditative melange of sonics: there are incantatory repetitions of words; the sounds modulate from louder sibilance in the first line ('so still') to flatter, deeper assonance in the last; and the ends of the poem's two sentences land with little onomatopoeic 't' sounds, 'almost' like the almost-sound of the dragonfly landing, where it 'almost' attaches to something humanmade. The poem, like the two preceding it, is a reminder that to notice such things – to gather 'anecdotal evidence', indeed – we must take our time and be as still as this 'still' day.

These three poems are followed by a run of ten about Shakespeare, or using him as a starting point. Nine are Shakespearean sonnets: an English version of another originally non-native form, applied to an English theme. Two engage specific sonnets of Shakespeare's, and reflect on the differences made – or not made – to our perceptions by modern scientific knowledge, the gathering of scientific rather than anecdotal evidence. The seven earlier poems in '*From* Strugnell's Sonnets' (*MC* 46–52), had each jostled with one or more Shakespearean counterpart. However, as with most of her earlier haiku, these had all been comical poems about misunderstanding. The newer poems about Shakespeare's sonnets are inquisitive, and often plaintive. 'On Sonnet 18' begins with the thirteenth line of that sonnet (Shakespeare, 147): '"So long as men can breathe and eyes can see" – / you don't assume we'll be around forever' (*AE* 34). Shakespeare could not have known that in a future time 'the sun goes supernova' – although here Cope seems to make her own scientific blunder by implying that humans will be around until that happens – but he did understand our time would be limited collectively, just as it is limited individually. In any case, the poem ends by questioning Shakespeare's professed certainty that his poem would endure: 'did you always know, or sometimes doubt, / That passing centuries would bear you out?' His performative bravado was not misplaced, but it did him no personal good.

Unlike 'On Sonnet 18', 'On Sonnet 22' is less a conversation with its antecedent and that poem's author than a separate meditation riffing off the same conceit, and in that sense has more in common with the aforementioned '*From* Strugnell's Sonnets'. It begins with a line almost identical to the one Shakespeare used to begin his poem: 'My glass shall not persuade me I am old' (Shakespeare, 155) becomes, in her counterpart, 'My glass can't quite persuade me I am old' (*AE* 41). Immediately, in the changed words, there is doubt where Shakespeare's speaker professed defiant certainty. The gulf between youth and age is made stark by dint of an invention Shakespeare did not have to contend with: 'when I see a photograph, I'm told / The dismal truth: I've left my youth behind.' However, Cope's poem is not addressed to a younger person, as is Shakespeare's, but to 'My love, who fell for me so long ago'. Ultimately, then, the poem offers recompense unavailable to Shakespeare's speaker: this is a love that has deepened as a direct result of the time that has caused both in this couple to age. Like 'each little trinket' in 'The Tree', old photographs are reminders, anecdotal evidence made concrete, of how far the couple have come, and the concomitant depth of their bond.

Near the end of *Anecdotal Evidence,* Cope includes several poems recalling the tones and themes of some of the wittier poems that were the mainstay of her earlier work. 'Where's a Pied Piper When You Need One?' is superficially reminiscent of 'A Hampshire Disaster' (*IIDK* 42), in that it riffs on a line from a newspaper – in this case, taking its title from a supposed headline in *The Daily Telegraph* on 25 May 2012.[11] The poem's conceit is simple: 'tourists flock to Hamelin' because of Robert Browning's *The Pied Piper of Hamelin,* even though they don't believe that poem's story that 'Thousands of rats are led to the river and to death by drowning', and they leave litter that, ironically, brings rats that 'gnaw through any cables that are lying around' (*AE* 56). The poem is in audacious rhymed couplets of unmetered verse, occasionally with consciously forced rhymes, in a manner that seems consciously to ape the dominant style of the most famous awful poet of them all, William McGonagall. The most audacious lines are perhaps saved for the end:

> The traffic lights stop working and so does the fountain.
> Council workers have repaired them so many times they
> have stopped countin',
>
> Which brings me at last to the burden of my song:
> Next time someone quotes Auden saying 'Poetry makes
> nothing happen', you can tell them he was wrong.

This is very mischievous. First, as it is self-consciously 'bad' verse, the allusions to two canonical poets (Browning and Auden) to make its point are comically indulgent. Second, Auden's line is not as straightforward as most (including the speaker) suppose, and can be read both as a simple declaration of the uselessness of poetry, and as the opposing statement, depending on how you emphasise it: 'poetry makes nothing *happen*'. Of course, as

Cope's poem points out, Browning's story of the Pied Piper is 'not a true one', so in a sense it has caused an event from 'nothing'. And, third, the story isn't unique to Browning's poem in any case, and in fact dates to at least the fourteenth century.

This run of witty – indeed, often light – poems includes 'Man Talking', which A. M. Juster describes as the book's 'one classic "Wendy Cope poem"',[12] seemingly because it is a pithy, tightly rhymed and metred poem of man-ribbing virility, and therefore ostensibly reminiscent of several poems in her first two collections. However, its mockery is relatively phlegmatic and comfortable, and less exasperated than its most obvious counterparts in those books. It is also, and unusually for Cope, in the second person, as though to infer that the experience it describes is probably also true to that of many readers. The presumably female speaker, whose presumably female second-person subject is stranded in the present tense with her thoughts while men tell 'Anecdotes and jokes, / On and on and on', claims:

> They'd notice, by and by,
> If you were to die.
>
> But it could take a while. (*AE* 58)

The imagined moment of their imagined noticing disappears over the line-break, as though to emphasise the imagined time lapse.

Perhaps it is fair to say this is an older person's take on male habits, and certainly this speaker seems more resigned to accepting apparently archetypal male behaviour than that of earlier poems such as 'I Worry', with its desire for men to suffer (*SC* 67). Moreover, in 'Men Talking', 'You neither speak nor smile' while it is going on, so the second-person subject remains passive when she might not have done so. 'At 70' is a more explicit take on age, and also harks back to her earlier tendencies for tight, humorous verse, although from the vantage of seniority. Like 'Where's a Pied Piper When You Need One?', it is in ludicrous rhymed couplets, although here they just about remain in heptameters, borrowed 'from Gilbert's lines about the "Major Gineral", / Where even Gilbert had to cheat to make it rhyme with mineral' (*AE* 60).[13] Cope uses the form to list off, frenetically, ailments and inconveniences attendant to ageing, and again takes stock:

> My blood tests came back fine when they were sent off for
> analysis.
> I'm lucky not to be on chemo or to need dialysis.
> My hips and knees are bearing up. They do not want replacing
> yet
> And cardiac anxieties are something I'm not facing yet. (*AE* 59)

The ludicrousness of the form is pointedly at odds with this serious checklist of things held off for now; the repetition of 'yet' implies it is only a matter of time. The poem is like a train hurtling down an incline: it is still on track, but one senses it is destined to careen off its rails at some point. This is funny, but it isn't exactly light. The poem bears up, and is glad not to have other anecdotal evidence to provide.

The book then ends with four poems that take us back to where it began, salutary reminders to treasure what we have had and what we have left, three of which refer to the importance of each 'day'. In the last of this book's many Shakespearean sonnets, 'New Year', as 'people party, set the sky ablaze', she mourns 'The passing of so many precious days' – the rhyme here reminding us that the days behind, like the fireworks, have burnt out (*AE* 63). As in Larkin's relentless later poem of death dread, 'Aubade' (Larkin, 115–16), some of the sentiments of which Cope had echoed in her earlier poem 'Once I'm Dead' (*FV* 28), each day serves to tell us 'we're nearer to the day we'll die', here signalled by the 'solemn midnight tolling', like a death knell, 'of Big Ben' (*AE* 63). There is no thematic turn in this sonnet, no 'But'; it ends with the speaker 'feeling old and sad', and the disconnection of sensing one is uniquely at odds with what seems to be 'the world [...] celebrating'.

In the next poem, 'Tallis's Canon', named for a piece of music included among Cope's choices when she appeared on *Desert Island Discs* in 2019,[14] she imagines attending her own funeral and 'singing my heart out: / *Keep me, O keep me, King of kings, / Beneath thine own almighty wings*' (*AE* 64) – although other poems in the book readily settle on atheism or agnosticism.[15] The pleasure comes from the singing, and the affirmation it gives of being alive, which makes the poem another reminder to live fully while you can. This is then interrogated through the lens of memory, rather than an imagined future, in the penultimate poem, 'Que Sera', which also involves the imagined rendering of song: the speaker and her father 'sang and sang' it 'in the car' when she was a child (*AE* 65). The poem's last line quotes the second line of that famous song chorus, '*What will be, will be*',[16] sandwiching the speaker's memory between these allusions, and coming as a daunting inevitability rather than a comforting philosophy. The poem plays sinisterly with the metaphor of life being a river: trying to 'organise / The future' is 'sculpting water'. However, unlike a river, as she goes metaphorically downstream, it moves 'faster every day' – a sentiment evoking the earlier 'Fireworks Poems' (*IIDK* 10). The only way to distract herself from this is to 'keep on humming': the title and the song are a distraction from facing up to the quixotic philosophy the song offers.

These poems of anguish are brought to an end, as is the book, with the short 'Every', written in October 2011, making it one of the earliest poems included in *Anecdotal Evidence*: Cope saved it for the send-off.[17] The poem uses its title as anaphora, anxiously and excitedly eschewing main verbs to focus on the object of each end-stopped line and sentence, and 'Every day that's left' (*AE* 66). All of these future days can provide, as the opening poem has it, further 'anecdotal evidence / About the human heart.'

6

'The gift of changing': Cope's Poems for Children

It is not surprising that a primary school teacher who became a poet for adults should also have become a poet for children, not least because she started writing poems while teaching, 'which involved doing a lot of creative work with children in music and poetry'.[1] Cope has written three books for young readers, all with a pedagogical function, and one more that is often regarded as a children's book, in addition to several other children's poems, some of which have appeared in anthologies. Elsewhere in this book, I have presented Cope's work chronologically, in sequence best to offer critical insight into her poetic development. In this chapter, however, I present her children's books in the order in which they are age-appropriate, in part to demonstrate her experiential understanding of encouraging children into what Lev Vygotsky called the 'zone of proximal development', and how she creatively marries this with an essential ingredient of all the easiest learning: fun.[2]

Twiddling Your Thumbs: Hand Rhymes (1988), Cope's earliest children's book, contains poems intended to suit children from the ages of two up to seven or eight. They are 'hand rhymes': poems with accompanying gestures, demonstrated in illustrations (by Sally Kindberg) on each page, and they originated in Cope's years working as a primary school teacher. As she writes in the introduction, 'A Note for Grown-Ups':

> The rhymes were originally written to be spoken aloud to nursery and infant classes, they never saw them written down. I asked the children to join in the actions. When they had heard a rhyme once or twice, they began to say the words with me as well. [...].

> Joining in action rhymes is a valuable part of a small child's musical education. (*TYT* 5)

The poems are all in forms that are likely to be familiar from school songs or rhymes: principally ballad metre ('Mary Had a Little Lamb' is also in this form, for example), although occasionally rhyming couplets of tetrameters or pentameters. They are suitably straightforward, but often offer pleasingly ingenious takes on childish staples, and imply the author was an inventive and pedagogically alert teacher. 'The Television', for example, is effectively peek-a-boo for children beyond earliest infancy. In eight lines of ballad metre and three finger gestures, we are encouraged to present a 'Quiet, dull' television screen (making a square with two hands, index finger to index finger, thumb to thumb), to turn it on with a twist, and then revert to the first gesture but so that it frames a nearby face:

> I'm looking at the television.
> Do you know who
> I can see in nice bright colours?
> I can see you! (*TYT* 15)

'In the Classroom' turns Georgie Porgie into a good boy who 'Put his hand up very high. / He didn't speak, he didn't shout / Because good children don't call out' (*TYT* 9). However, the illustration shows two hungry wolves in cook's aprons carrying off a pie, out of which a boy's arm protrudes vertically. We are therefore encouraged to raise our arm in accompaniment to the poem, imagine we are Georgie in the pie, and perhaps mischievously cotton on to the notion that being one of the 'good children' isn't necessarily always the best idea, whatever the adults might tell us.

In her 'Note' to the book, Cope adds that 'graded schemes may have their place but the really important thing is to learn to love books'. Two more recent commissions show Cope attempting to create loveable poems in keeping with a graded scheme. The first, and her other book for very young people, *Time for School* (2013), comprises one poem of sixteen lines, spread across twelve pages. It is part of the Collins Big Cat series, intended to help children 'become fluent readers through [...] banded books by top authors and illustrators'.[3] The book is aimed at younger schoolchildren, and belongs to 'band 3' in their scheme, described by Collins as follows:

- Repetition of phrase patterns, ideas and vocabulary [...].
- Storylines include episodes in a time sequence and framework of familiar experiences.
- Some literary conventions, familiar oral language structures, illustrations support the text quite closely. (Collins Big Cat website)

The poem is conventional fare, but perfectly fits the remit. It is in rhymed couplets of tetrameters, a form used in many nursery rhymes such as 'Humpty Dumpty' or 'Baa Baa Black Sheep', and therefore almost certain to be instinctively familiar to any child of primary school age. It follows a supposedly typical school day, complemented by Mike Phillips's colourful illustrations, most of which show a classroom clock, and all of which owe something to Quentin Blake in composition and characterful scruffiness. The poem repeats inverted phrases at mirrored positions in the text, giving the day it portrays a neatly rounded narrative arc: 'work and play' in the fourth line becomes 'More play, more work' in the fourth-from-last, and the opening couplet ends 'Hello teacher. Bye-bye Mum', whereas the final one ends 'Bye-bye teacher, hello Mum' (*TFS* 3, 12, 2, and 3, respectively). The school day is presented as a uniformly joyous routine, with 'friends' (*TFS* 3) and an equal emphasis on the apparently equally fun tasks of playing and learning. Aside from break and lunch times, the day's activities are summed up in the couplet 'Books to read and sums to do, / Stories, painting pictures too' (*TFS* 4–5), and then 'We sing' (*TFS* 10). Cope therefore subtly implies that a young child's interests are best served by centring opportunities for individual and collective creativity. It is delightful to read this utterly innocent poem in the full knowledge of how Cope played with the format of an educational reader in 'Reading Scheme' (*MC* 7), but this is a serious commission taken seriously, and fulfils its intended pedagogical function while also offering a tacit recommendation to educators, and an encouragement to children to enjoy themselves.

Going for a Drive (2010) is a volume of twenty short illustrated rhyming poems in multiple simple metrically formal styles. This book is in the same series as *Time for School,* but is for more advanced 'band 7' readers, the intended 'learning opportunities' for whom include navigating 'around texts' and using 'punctuation and text layout to read with expression and control' (Collins Big Cat website). The former skill is emphatically necessary in the final poem, 'A poetry journey – from morning till night', which follows a road up the verso and down and across the recto of a double-page spread, and therefore requires readers to cotton on to not reading in the conventional top-left to bottom-right manner (*GFD* 22–3). The short collection also includes several poems requiring implicit and learned understandings of layout and punctuation. 'Boo!' is especially noteworthy in this regard. Each of the poem's four stanzas uses the same metre, opening word, and fourth line:

> If I see the big bad wolf,
> I know what to do.
> There's a word that I must say:
> BOO! (*GFD* 18)

The poem is therefore almost in ballad stanzas, and Cope also uses ballad stanzas in five other poems in this volume, three of which appear earlier in the book. However, the monosyllabic last word of this poem is obviously far from being the metrically required line of trimeter. The capitalisation and exclamation mark, coupled with a reader's innate and reinforced predilection for repeating patterns, encourage the space to be filled in with a performatively loud and elongated 'BOO-OO-OO!'

The book also contains 'Summer Haiku', which subtly introduces children to the fuller workings of a familiar form:

> Shimmering heat waves –
> A hot pebble in the hand,
> Light-dance on the sea. (*GFD* 13)

There is more to a haiku than counting syllables, of course, although that is often all children are taught about them at school. Cope also adheres to the other requirements of the form, implying a season and bringing together two images.[4]

The poem 'Kenneth (who was too fond of bubble-gum and met an untimely end)' has not been collected, but is popular in anthologies, so bears discussion here.[5] This cautionary tale is one of three Cope wrote in the 1980s,[6] and owes a huge intertextual debt to Hilaire Belloc's 'Henry King', from which it borrows much in terms of both phrasing and plot. 'The chief defect of Henry King', writes Belloc,

> Was chewing little bits of string.
> At last he swallowed some which tied
> Itself in ugly knots inside.[7]

Cope's Kenneth has a slightly more common and contemporary addiction: 'The chief defect of Kenneth Plumb / Was chewing too much bubble-gum' (McGough, 25). Both boys get their respective addictive materials stuck in their systems, and are taken to doctors, who prognose imminent death (in Belloc's case, 'as they took their fees', a dig at the apparent proclivities of some in the pre-National Health Service medical establishment), which transpires. The ironic pun on Kenneth Plumb's name is a nice touch, because if he could have been plumbed he might have survived. Belloc's poem ends with Henry, immediately before he 'expires', warning others to learn from his example, but Cope leaves out Kenneth's final moments and provides the valedictory warning through the narrator, in a couplet separated emphatically from the main stanza: 'Remember Ken, and please do not / Go buying too much you-know-what.' Both poems are simply too comically ludicrous to be taken seriously, but Cope's change to Belloc's ending is a kind of bowdlerisation that ensures the focus of her poem is more on comical excess than its wicked consequences, and her poem is the longer of the two, including more examples of his dedication to chewing, in a manner more reminiscent of Roald Dahl's poems for children.

Cope's longest poem – for adults or children – is *The River Girl*, published in 1991. I include this book-length poem in this chapter cautiously, and with a caveat. The Movingstage Marionette Company, who commissioned it, did not request a children's poem. Moreover, it contains what might be considered adult topics and language. Certainly, it is thick with Cope's then-prevalent themes – explored at some length in *Serious*

Concerns – of love-longing and disappointment, not least in its philosophical asides. Moreover, it is wittily dismissive of the failings of needy poets and the world of small, acrimonious literary parties: in one aside she notes that such gatherings and conversations drive her 'round the bend // And I'm supposed to *be* a poet' (*RG* 28), and elsewhere she shows a poet drunkenly referring to an editor as a 'bastard' for failing to publish him (*RG* 36). These might not only be regarded as adult matters, but also ones confined to a small proportion of adults, even though most children have no trouble seeing through the stupidity of grown-ups or coping with some rudeness. In any case, Faber marketed it as a book for children, and its fairy-tale-like narrative does make it more appropriate for a younger audience than most of the poems in her five main collections.[8]

The River Girl is another cautionary tale in formal verse, this time composed entirely in iambic pentameter quatrains rhyming ABCB – a form not far removed from that used seven years earlier by Tony Harrison for his similarly lengthy poem 'v.',[9] and one perfectly suited to carrying a long, conversational narrative. Throughout, Cope maintains a form of alternating feminine and masculine endings, the extra syllable in the first and third lines of each quatrain adding a lilt that can be lyrical, as below, or comical, as in some of the later examples in this chapter. It begins by setting the scene – 'a stream' in Gloucestershire, an early section of Britain's second mightiest river:

> [...] it meets the ocean
> A mighty thoroughfare, deep, wide and strong.
> It knew our forbears. It will know our children.
> *Sweet Thames run softly till I end my song.* (*RG* 4)

Of course, that last line (slightly mis-)quotes a repeated line from T. S. Eliot's *The Waste Land*, and Eliot's intertext at that point of his poem, Edmund Spenser's 'Prothalamion':[10] the river has been flowing just the same through all iterations, and will continue to do so. It stretches behind and before us – temporally, but also geographically, in that it almost bisects England. Spenser's poem depicts a wedding by a pastoral, idyllic Thames, against which Eliot sets the more modern, littered river, on which we later see an unromantic tryst: 'By Richmond I raised my knees / Supine on the floor of a narrow canoe' (Eliot, 34). Cope's poem retreats far upstream to discover a contemporary riverside idyll, and return the line to a depiction of courtship, marriage, and what follows marriage – although that comes later, as we shall see.

On the riverbank there is another eternality, at least of the Anthropocene: a 'would-be poet, seeking inspiration', who 'dreams of greatness'. The rewards he seeks are extrinsic, not intrinsic – but soon he has his 'inspiration' in the form of the poem's female hero: 'the lovely Isis, / Giver of dreams, enchantress, river girl' (*RG* 5), who lives beneath the river. Her name plays on that of the Ancient Egyptian goddess, indeed a giver of eternal dreams, believed to help people enter the afterlife. However, the name is also shared with the upper portion of the Thames, where the narrative takes place: she is both the river *girl*, and the river *incarnate*, eternal, and not to be mastered, however much we might bend nature to our will. On the other hand, he is a vain mortal, and apparently unobservant – not an ideal trait in a poet – for 'Isis sees' him first.

This might remind readers of some of Cope's laments about certain men in *Serious Concerns*, which was nearing completion when *The River Girl* was published, and at this point the narrative is interrupted by an aside that is essentially a phlegmatic precis of what was for her, at that time, a recurring theme: love is described as 'a fast-moving current / That seizes us before we've time to think', and 'some of us it carries on to safety / Upon a happy shore, while others sink'.[11] Isis, it seems, has been thus 'seized', but it is immediately evident that the object of her affections is a bit of a fool:

> 'Your hair will dry and gleam like finest satin.
> I'll gather flowers and make a little crown
> And place it on your head and call you "Princess" –
> Good heavens. Hang on. I must write this down.'
>
> He lets her go and scribbles in his notebook.
> A miracle! He is in love and *writing*. (*RG* 7)

He can't be 'in love': they have just met. However, rather than wallow in this giddily romantic insanity, he is overwhelmed by a desire to get a poem out of the moment he prevents himself from having. Moreover, his new-found lines, such as 'My love is like the first light of the dawn' and 'My love is like a rose without a thorn' (*RG* 8) – the latter uncannily resembling and reversing the sentiment of Poison's 1988 hit single 'Every Rose Has its Thorn' – are clichéd doggerel.[12]

Isis then leaves 'the world we know', and the next section of the poem follows her to 'the kingdom underwater / That's ruled by Father Thames' (*RG* 11). He is also her father, 'part pantomime myth-Dad, and part suburban father of a teenaged girl', as Atar Hadari puts it.[13] He 'dreads the day some other love will beckon / And call his Isis to the world above' (*RG* 12), but has the magical power to 'confer the gift of changing', allowing her to transform into 'any living thing' (*RG* 16) such as a land-dwelling human. She tells him that she has met 'the one for me', and that 'if I'm not with him, I think I'll die' (*RG* 15) – the kind of overblown statement that immediately testifies to her youth. When she tells him that the object of her desire is a poet, he 'sighs. It's worse than he expected' – but ultimately he grants her wish, letting her make her own mistakes.

Impulse is not a good basis for lasting love. The next section takes us forward six months, to find 'our lovers' already married and living together 'in a little flat', where he 'writes and writes' and she does 'The cooking and the housework' (*RG* 20). The magical river girl is reduced to a functional supporting role, while a very average man gets to pursue his worldlier dreams. She inspires his poems, though, and he gets taken on by the publisher Tite and Snobbo, and 'that famed poet, / Tite's editor, the dreaded Clinton Thunder' (*RG* 22). This is a cheeky joke at the expense of her publisher Faber & Faber, those two names replaced by ones redolent of pretension, and her editor Craig Raine, a 'famed poet', whose first name also begins with a C and whose second name is also (at least as a homophone) a type of bad weather.[14] In *Making Cocoa for Kinglsey Amis,* as we have seen, she had parodied Raine's poetry in 'The Lavatory Attendant' (*MC* 39); here, she pokes fun at his profession, playfully chomping at the hand that feeds her, while simultaneously sending up an archetype, as is common in children's narratives.[15] In any case, the as-yet-unnamed poet-lover – for he is a kind of everyman everypoet – is delighted, and runs to kiss 'My Muse, my love, my life, my inspiration' (*RG* 24). These words are undoubtedly true, and portentous.

In the next section of the poem, we find him 'in demand' and garlanded with awards for his new book. We also, finally, learn his name: 'He's called John Didde. That's D-I-D-D-E, yes, / A little like John Donne' (*RG* 27). His name is indeed redolent of this Renaissance poet of love-longing, which encourages us to see him as a pale, modish counterpart – and, forebodingly, his name puts him in the past tense, as though all his achievements are behind him by the time we learn it.

This is another portent: Didde is caught up in his success, and forgets his muse and love. Trapped at one of many literary parties, she longs 'to be at home, away from all these people. / Though, even there, things aren't quite what they were' (*RG* 28). She goes to see her father, back in the river, to ask his advice, and he greets her with a string of questions: 'how's your poet?' Is he 'Loving, kind and faithful? / Treating his lovely wife the way he should? / Behaving better than the other poets?' (*RG* 33). The answers, of course, are a string of negatives, and she returns to her husband intent on giving him one more chance. She is suffering. But so is Didde's art, now he has forgotten to attend to his Muse. At one party, a woman to whom he gets too close ('The others watch. Is something going on?') asks him what he is writing: 'Not much. Some days the output's nil'. His 'output' (trust him to use a business term for his poetry) is 'slowing down' (*RG* 37). Without his wife, he would not have had success in his chosen art; by then privileging his success in art over his wife, he stands to lose both. Perhaps sensing he is on the verge of infidelity, his forgotten wife remembers her bestowed ability to shape-shift, and disturbs them, in the guise of a 'vicious' cat. It is a misplaced cry for help, from a woman who wants 'some attention' (*RG* 40).

This precipitates the bitter-sweet end. The next morning he tells her he is going to London and she snaps, exasperated at again being forgotten, and calls upon her powers once more to turn into a 'snarling' cat (*RG* 43). Unable to find his wife, and keen to be off, he locks it in a basket and scribbles a note to Isis asking her to get rid of it. As such, he accidentally buries her alive, because she has kept something from him, too. His self-absorption is his downfall; her dishonesty risks being hers – although again she calls on her powers, transforms into a swallow, and literally and symbolically pushes her way out and flies 'free' as a bird, back to the river (*RG* 46). As she stands on the riverbank, back where she met the would-be poet, and prepares to 'disappear' from our world, she has 'her head held high' (*RG* 49): by leaving, she has done the right thing, and she knows it. The poem, then, ultimately shows the moral value and benefit of knowing when a relationship is no longer working, and having the self-respect and strength to extricate oneself. It ends with Didde alone and 'Tormented by self-hatred' as he 'walks along the river / Day after day' to 'this place, where they first met' (*RG* 50). In a future time, we are told, we might 'chance to find / A copy of his book': he did only write one, it seems, and John Didde really was John who *did* but no longer *does*.

This is a poem about a remarkable woman's ultimate dignity and growth in a world favourable to unremarkable men, and serves as a cautionary tale about the cost of failing to cherish those who have helped you become what you are. And, like the flowing river with which the poem begins and ends, its less fantastical paralogues will repeat indefinitely. A good poem for children need have no upper age limit, and this is a lesson for all ages.

7

'They waited patiently': Uncollected Cope

In 2019, Cope said that 'Quite a lot' of what she has written has not been included in her books, adding that she has many uncollected poems 'that I now think are not too bad'.[1] Some found publication in pamphlets in the 1980s,[2] but were left out of her first two collections; others have got no further than typescript. It is Cope's intention to produce a *Collected Poems* including previously uncollected poems,[3] and mine in this chapter to provide an insight into some of them, and their points of connection or divergence with poems in her collections. In order to do this most effectively, I approach these uncollected poems, as far as seems sensible, in chronological order – ending with critical comment on work written or published since *Anecdotal Evidence,* and where her poetry appears to be heading.

Cope's notebooks don't reveal true juvenilia: she was in her late twenties when she started to write poetry. Almost all of her earliest unpublished poems are in free verse, and none exhibit the wit frequently found in her first two collections. They only provide occasional indications of her later modes, typically in notions of promise gilding despair. For example, in 'Friday Night', dated '9/3/73', it is 'Time to breathe easy' and imagine 'A yellow plain' with a geyser, where 'bubbles rise / and calmly burst' and 'warm water laps the earth'.[4] A haiku-like poem with a comparable moral, dated '16/6/73', reads: ''Yes! He still glows. / This mist-bound firefly. / But the world is cold and grey.'[5] These early pieces do not sound much like the published Cope, but the same spirit of desolation and determination lies behind later poems such as 'The Aerial', where it is married with concrete human experience, and after she has developed the characteristically snappier style that helped make her name.

Stronger signs of that style become instantly more apparent in the late 1970s. 'Going Away', completed in 1978, is an apparently autobiographical poem that has much in common with the plain-spoken poems about childhood Cope would later include in *Family Values*, although nothing like it appeared in her collections before her mother's death in 2004:

> On the platform where the school train left,
> Seven years old, she didn't cry
> But smiled and chattered
> Like the schoolgirls she had met in books,
> Kissed her parents and went away.
> She never really came back.[6]

The childhood poems in *Family Values* consider such circumstances from the vantage point of late middle age, which has for Cope been a time of relative contentment. However, this much earlier poem has an unsettling timbre unique among her poems on this subject, ushered in by that final line of the first stanza: this speaker is a woman who is still searching for home, who can pinpoint the distant beginning of this search to that moment on the departing train, and who still 'knows that every love / will end in brave farewell', as she puts it in the third and final stanza. By using the third person – a point of view Cope would only adopt for two of the nine poems about childhood in *Family Values* – the speaker distances herself semantically from the human subject she describes, as though looking at her objectively, trapped on a circuit.

At about the same time, she drafted two other poems about her parents, both in the first person. Both imply repression, but also love. 'My Father', an elegy with phrases repeated like waves of grief, begins with an epigraph from Marina Tsvetaeva: 'Let me sing of sorrow / from the top of the mountains'.[7] Cope's poem is about not being able to do so when he died: 'We always tried to hide our sorrows, / Knowing / The other's pain', and then 'We always tried to hide our sorrows, / And with them our love'.[8] 'Hiding Place', by contrast, is jocular as well as tense, although that tension again comes from the speaker feeling she has something to hide when she doesn't. Her mother cleans the daughter's kitchen while the latter is sick, but promises not to look in the oven: 'What's / in the oven?', Cope's speaker wonders, as 'Old guilts come gallivanting / Back', the notion of them returning highlighted by being held over the line-break. Then:

> It couldn't be *The Joy*
> *Of Sex*, not in the oven.
> No, I'm certain
> That one's hidden in a drawer.[9]

'Perhaps', she concludes with a metaphorical flourish, she 'Doesn't mind / What's in my cupboards'. Perhaps their relationship can be open and equal now. It makes an intriguing counterpart to her later poems about home life in *Family Values*, where such softer possibilities have conclusively been vanquished.

Cope has said that she has often avoided publishing poems that might upset people (*Desert Island Discs*), and none of these made it into her first pamphlet, *Across the City* (1980), published by Priapus Press. Priapus was run by John Cotton, with the aim of providing 'a platform for new poetry and poets',[10] and had developed from *Priapus* (1963–72), a magazine with a reputation for printing early work by poets who would go on to develop significant reputations, such as John Mole, Peter Scupham, and D. M. Thomas. Greater success for Cope soon followed when twenty of her poems were included in Faber's *Poetry Introduction 5* anthology in 1982.[11] Most of these would reappear in her debut collection, *Making Cocoa for Kingsley Amis*, but seven would not. These include her first published Christmas poem, 'Christmas Triolet' – the pithiest of light verse, without any of the sting of her finer Christmas poems, although it does demonstrate significant formal panache in its use of repetends, in which 'merry carols' in the second line is replaced by 'merry Carol's' drunken fate at the end of the poem (*PI* 21).[12] More intriguing are 'Thaw' (also included in *Across the City*) and 'Flowering Cherries', both of which are unique in her published work for anthropomorphising trees in extended conceits.[13] In the former, the speaker is 'Under trees' that are 'Like aged priests', 'baptising us' as the ice melts (*PI* 24). She is young in their eternal-seeming presence. Moreover, she is not alone: this is a shared, treasured moment. 'Flowering Cherries', on the other hand, is not a poem about rebirth, but another one about natural fortitude, and the speaker is a non-participant observer. These cherries 'are street trees / And they'll bear no fruit' (*PI* 23). Nonetheless, 'every year / They swell with blossom' and 'dream that they are pregnant'. Cope was childless at thirty-seven when this poem was published, and it is tempting to read a ticking biological clock into the poem. In any case, as Don Paterson puts it in his more recent poem 'Two Trees', 'trees don't weep or ache or shout',[14] let alone dream. By fancifully proclaiming that they do, Cope draws attention to the opposite – and the fact that people do have desires they might not fulfil, potentially including the desire to rear children.

The inclusion of Cope's poetry in *Poetry Introduction 5* initiated a relationship with Faber that has endured. Her selection in that anthology also introduced in book format her alter-ego, Jake or Jason Strugnell, in poems such as 'Mr Strugnell' and 'Strugnell Haiku', and her early penchant for lampooning living male poets, in 'Budgie Finds His Voice' (*MC* 37), a parody of fellow Faber poet Ted Hughes in his *Crow* phase, and 'The Lavatory Attendant' (*MC* 39), a delightfully mischievous parody of her new editor at Faber, Craig Raine. In 1985, when Cope's debut collection *Making Cocoa for Kingsley Amis* was in preparation, her new publisher printed a promotional pamphlet containing five poems from the forthcoming book and 'The Desmond Clarke Poem', which has never been reprinted because, according to Cope, 'Craig [Raine, her editor] said it was too incestuous. I think he was right.'[15] The poem is named for the then-marketing director of the company, and bears an epigraph from him: 'We are to poetry what Mills and Boon are to romance'.[16] The speaker, 'a lonely housewife' – the stereotypical audience for escapist trash fiction – likes nothing better than to 'curl up with a sherry and devour the latest Faber', instead of with 'thrilling tales of lust and passion': 'So you can keep your tall, dark heroes, Messrs Mills and Boon'. Clearly, this is a joke aimed at her publisher's attitude towards selling poetry, as well as at the notion that the poetry world is full of men who are romantic 'heroes'. The poem is partly a joke at her own expense, too, because now she is among that company in Faber covers. It is a bold, witty move, and one that would manifest in many less 'incestuous' poems in her debut.

However, other parodies and literary jokes were also dropped from that book. *Hope and the 42*, a pamphlet published in 1984, included 'abridged' versions of D. H. Lawrence's *Lady Chatterley's Lover* (in a couplet), and Chaucer's 'The Man of Law's Tale', which gives up at the end in a line of absurd exegesis: 'The goodies triumphed and the baddies died'.[17] These foreshadow her abbreviation of T. S. Eliot in 'Waste Land Limericks' (*MC* 10), which she did include in her first book. Moreover, Strugnell's public oeuvre might have been larger than it is. An uncollected Strugnell poem from the early 1980s, 'The Ballade of Jason Strugnell', joins two poems included in *Making Cocoa for Kingley Amis* by using Eliot for sport. Here, we find Strugnell at his most self-pitying, comparing himself to 'lucky sod' Prufrock, because 'I'm melancholy as a man can be'.[18] Although it shares little in terms of form with 'The Love Song of J. Alfred Prufrock', Cope's poem does bastardise some of Eliot's most famous lines to reveal other sides to Strugnell's character, which might now remind a reader of Alan Partridge: 'In the room the women start anew / Their talk of endless struggles to be free'. To Strugnell, this is nothing but an unwelcome distraction from his pathetic attempt to demonstrate himself the *poète maudit par excellence*.

Cope also left out of her debut collection several sonnets once intended for the sequence '*From* Strugnell's Sonnets': her archive contains four beyond the seven in *Making Cocoa for Kingsley Amis*. Some tread on the toes of what she does better in the included poems, or are too tame. One apes 'Shall I compare thee to a summer's day?' without sufficiently moving away from its intertext, other than to have him confess 'I could be wrong' at the end;[19] another warns 'fellow bards' to 'stick to orange juice before you read'.[20] Better is 'When in disgrace with fortune and the boss', which plays with Shakespeare's 'Sonnet 29'[21] to find Strugnell opening his heart to 'the barmaid' (not '*a* barmaid' – he is a regular) about having his poems returned 'From *Lemons* or *The Crazy Frog* or *Sludge*', three deliciously accurate-seeming fictitious names for third-rate literary magazines.[22] The best unpublished Strugnell sonnet, though, is the riotously inappropriate 'When in the chronicle of wasted rhyme', riffing on the opening line of Shakespeare's 'Sonnet 106' (Shakespeare, 323), in which he reads sordid accounts from 'randy poets who are past their prime':

Then, reeling at their use of words so bold
As cunt, or anus, not to mention fuck,
I long to have such stories to unfold.[23]

He concludes, 'Perhaps I'll make it up, for who could tell? / Perhaps the others make it up as well.' Strugnell naturally would hope so – but nowhere else in 'his' poems is he 'bold' enough to use those words, and nowhere else in his life is he likely to have cause for them. Moreover, he unwittingly blurs the distinction between these three apparent vulgarisms: excessiveness ('not to mention') is implied for the less offensive of the two swear words, and 'anus' is a scientific, non-vulgar term that it is probably safe to say nobody has ever used in bed.

Strugnell, who was invented in the late 1970s by Cope in collusion with the novelist and poet D. M. Thomas (whose counterpart was 'Fred Pushkin'),[24] began life as an entrant to poetry competitions in places such as the *New Statesman* and *The Spectator*, his name above Cope's address at the foot of each poem. She also entered one to *The Spectator* as 'Penny Whistle', from the same address, shortly after the publication of *Making Cocoa for Kingsley Amis*. Penny Whistle hates poets: 'A pox on every twisted bore', she writes,

Who thinks he's William Blake
And hates our guts if we ignore
His lyric bellyache.[25]

To an eagle-eyed editor at *The Spectator*, it might have appeared that she 'lives' with Strugnell, a poet *manqué* keen to make a self-important fumble at any poet's style, and is struggling with him. It is tempting, therefore, to read her as another persona. However, Cope notes that she used the name 'to remain anonymous', and that the poem expresses 'my feelings at the time', after her debut had been attacked by some in the literary press.[26]

By 1988, when she published the short pamphlet *Does She Like Word-Games?*, Cope had become one of the best-selling poets in the Anglosphere.[27] This pamphlet begins with one of her most acerbic and sweeping parodies, 'Three Contemporary Poets', which has not been included in any subsequent books, but that in part continues the witty ribbing of her new publisher. Each of its three sections is a closely observed pastiche, comprising a biographical note for an invented contemporary poet, and then a very short example of his or her work. The first is one Liam Doonican, who 'grew up on a turnip farm in County Armagh' but who 'now lives in Ealing', and whose collections '*Mud* (Faber, 1981) and *Root Vegetables* (Faber, 1984) have established him as one of the twenty-eight most outstanding talents to emerge from Ireland in recent years' (*DSL* 3). This is an unfocused attack on Northern Irish poets who emerged in Heaney's wake, as well as the major publisher who, it is implied, faddishly gave some of their work (and Heaney's) a home. Now presumably working towards his third collection, Doonican's themes do not seem to have developed, for his poem is about mud and root vegetables. It also owes something, admittedly, to Heaney's 'Sunlight', although in Doonican's poem it is, more characteristically, 'raining'. The images, too, are Heaneyesque, if Heaney hadn't known what he was doing and had tumbled into ludicrousness, for the turnips are remembered as 'an underground brigade / Stacked in [Grandfather's] creaking tumbril': 'They waited patiently / Outside the kitchen door / For father's sharpened knife'. One wonders what an impatient turnip looks like.

The second poet, Nigel Courcy-Denton (b. 1948), 'is the son of a Weybridge stock-broker', attended Oxford, and is now 'married, with two children, and lives in Highgate', an extremely expensive part of London, where he 'works as a freelance journalist and broadcaster'. This is all quite an achievement for a man in his early thirties, although one suspects he has had a well-polished run to success. His poem is an exercise in showing off, an example of that common scourge Cope has derided as 'lifestyle poetry',[28] devoid of tension, with in this case needless references to accoutrements such as 'the cork-tiled floor', and 'Our children and their kittens'. The third poet, Jasmine Gladyschild, probably wouldn't have much time for the likes of Courcy-Denton, for she 'was born in 1946 and reborn in 1974 when she became part of the Women's Movement'. She seems to be a poet of little success beyond this circle, where she has 'contributed to the feminist anthology *Pearls and Swine*', and she appears to be an academic or independent scholar of the activist stripe, who is 'working on a study of crèche facilities in women's publishing collectives'. Her poem is a simplistic, abstracted cry of anguish, and an apparently unwitting admission that she can't write: 'i want / to express myself / in words' and 'tell you / about love, pain, anger, joy', but 'find it difficult'.

Pearls and Swine does not exist, but has contemporaneous counterparts such as the anthology *One Foot on the Mountain* (1979). This includes work by Aspen Joycechild Womun, a poet with a name strikingly similar to Cope's invention, who writes a poem with a sentiment not unlike Jasmine Gladyschild's, at least in part, and with similarly insistent use of uncapitalised first-person pronouns: 'i cry out / all you hear is a moan on the wind / [...] i insist you pay attention'.[29] Cope's poem, however, has more in common with the third part of Lesley Sanders's 'Voices', from the same anthology, the speaker of which is apparently, and somehow, a new-born child: 'I cannot make words / my mouth / can only cry' (*One Foot*, 137). Cope mischievously puts sentiments akin to those given to a baby directly in the voice of her invented feminist poet – who, of course, should have some talent for applying language to her purposes.

It is worth pointing out that Cope's earlier poetry especially often spoke out against male entitlement. *The River Girl* (1991), for example, can be read as a whole book about it. Moreover, the year after 'Three Contemporary Poets' was published, she edited an anthology of women poets, the introduction for which extols the virtues of 'excluding men, now and again'.[30] The year before, she had described herself as 'a feminist', albeit one who couldn't abide 'goddess-worshipping' feminism.[31] In 2013, she reiterated that she is 'a feminist [...] who believes men and women are equal', and in the mid-2000s she wrote the BBC-commissioned 'On Dipping Into a Feminist Dictionary', an alphabetical poem apparently written with tongue only occasionally in cheek, in which 'C' is for 'Consciousness of what we've all put up with', and 'X is for the chromosomes of which we have a pair / And Y's the one you need if you're to be a son and heir'.[32] The third part of 'Three Contemporary Poets' is not anti-feminist to anyone not desperate to find it so: it mocks literary banality and – like the two other parts of the poem – the poetic pretension of thinking you have something to say when you don't.

These parodies lack the precise, studied single victims of some of their counterparts in *Making Cocoa for Kingsley*

Amis. However, they do lampoon genuine tendencies in the more modish poetries of the 1970s and 1980s. Moreover, the short sequence is economically vengeful in its breadth: it is a scatter-gun rather than a blunderbuss. Cope notes, 'When *Making Cocoa* was published, with huge publicity and huge sales, a lot of poets were envious and spiteful [but] had comfortable lives, nice homes, and families, i.e. everything I wanted. That was hard to take.'[33] She has also said that when she was a young poet, 'if you called yourself a feminist writer, other feminists would give you a hard time if they didn't think you were feminist enough'.[34] Ultimately, the poem is an act of revenge on those who had shunned her; but she opted not to give this revenge space in a collection, and instead increasingly turned her attention away from parodies of poets.

There were a few more, though, in *Men and Their Boring Arguments*, another pamphlet published in 1988. 'Wordsworth's Ode on Intimations of Mortality from recollections of early Childhood (abridged)' (*MBA*) plays on its comically prolix title by matching it to four tiny rhyming couplets of phlegmatic bathos, very unlike Wordsworth in everything but subject, in which we learn that 'To a mite / Things look bright', but 'Still, must say / I'm OK'.[35] Another parody, 'Strugnell's Bargain', essentially takes the same idea as '*From* Strugnell's Sonnets', but riffs on Sir Philip Sidney's 'Heart Exchange',[36] rather than Shakespeare:

> My true love hath my heart and I have hers:
> We swapped last Tuesday and felt quite elated.
> But now, whenever one of us refers
> To 'my heart', things get rather complicated. (*MBA*)

The hapless Strugnell does what we might expect of him, and corrects his love's mistakes with what Stephen Regan calls 'farcical literal-mindedness'.[37] Eventually, sick of this man's boring arguments, she tells him to 'piss off', which leads to a self-pitying sestet in which he takes his bat and ball home with him: 'I revoke my opening line. / My love can keep her heart and I'll have mine'. Thus, the poem ends with a *volte face*, rather than the reiteration of the first line provided by Sidney, and Strugnell has lost his love rather than confirmed it. This is almost as witty as anything in '*From* Strugnell's Sonnets', but

Cope had been dissuaded from collecting it because she rhymes 'kidney' and 'Sidney' and Raine pointed out that Eliot had used the same rhyme.[38]

Men and Their Boring Arguments also contains 'Ever So Cute' (*MBA;* previously included in *Hope and the* 42), another poem very much in the vein of the parodies in her debut book. This is a modernised counterpart to A. A. Milne's cutesy 'Vespers' (1924), truncated from six quatrains to four, and made brutal. The two poems are at their closest, lexically, in their first stanzas. Milne's begins:

> Little Boy kneels at the foot of the bed,
> Droops on the little hands little gold head.
> Hush! Hush! Whisper who dares!
> Christopher Robin is saying his prayers.[39]

Cope steals the third line but gives it a very different application, because her Christopher Robin will batter you if you aren't careful:

> Little boy dressed in his white judo suit,
> Little black belt looking ever so cute.
> Hush! Hush! Whisper who dares!
> Christopher Robin can throw you downstairs.

Milne's Christopher Robin is quick to 'bless' his parents for simple pleasures such as having 'fun in the bath'. But Milne's 'God bless Mummy' becomes 'Go on Mummy, it's only ten – / I want to watch "Dracula's Bride" again' (and the cajoling seems to have a history of paying off, because 'Me and my teddy like violence and sex'). Milne's 'God bless Daddy', on the other hand, is replaced with a desire to 'kill' more enemies than 'Dad' in a 'video game', 'when [the film is] over' – after midnight, in other words, when Milne's Christopher Robin would be fast asleep with his good Christian dreams.

Fewer of Cope's completed poems remain uncollected after the 1980s: like most poets, she has become more assured over time at deciding what to abandon. However, there are some fine uncollected poems from the past thirty years, some of which shed light on her collected work. These include 'Unwritten Rules', from the mid-1990s, a perfectly rhymed and metrical villanelle about how 'full rhyme's a little bit suspect today': 'It's important to write in an up-to-date way / And I trust it is clear that I know where it's at'.[40] The poem is essentially an ironised counterpart to the less specified 'The Ted Williams Villanelle', which encourages the reader not to let anyone 'mess with your swing', and which she included in her next collection (*IIDK* 35).

'Unwritten Rules' seeks to disprove its ostensible point by flouting its own argument. This is a tactic Cope had earlier employed in 'An Attempt at Unrhymed Verse', written in 1985. This poem is not in any of her collections, although she reads it publicly, beginning her Poetry Archive recording with the poem as though it is a manifesto she intends to flout, and she included it in her *Selected Poems* (*TCL* 72).[41] It begins by saying that she is often told poems needn't rhyme: 'Often it's better if they don't /And I'm determined this one won't. / Oh dear.'[42] In the second stanza, she writes:

> Never mind. I'll start again –
> Busy, busy with my pen...cil.
> I can do it if I try –
> Easy, peasy, pudding and gherkins.

However, in an earlier draft, that final word was 'pie...crust'. In the abandoned version, then, she continues to make the 'mistake' or rhyming because it works, skewering her rhyming words. The final version, on the other hand, shows the speaker 'improving' at following the instruction of those keen to mess with her swing: in the first stanza she accidentally rhymes anyway, in the next two lines she learns to catch herself at the last moment, and then she wises up to avoiding rhyme altogether. By the end of the poem, a quatrain later, she has gone beyond this education to embrace the prolix avoidance of metre, too, in which the obvious word choice, 'right', is jettisoned in favour of 'more or less the way you want it' – which is not the same thing, as well as being a very positive take on how this increasingly ludicrous poem ends up. These aren't two of her finer poems, but they very effectively make the point that we are instinctively drawn to prosodic repetitions and, in any case, sometimes avoiding them is more cumbersome than not doing so. While they sit outside her collected work, they certainly speak to her decision predominantly to use rhyme and metre through the 1980s and 1990s.

In the late 1980s and early 1990s, Cope translated three poems by the German Heinrich Heine,[43] a poet from whom she would soon take a line in her poem 'The Lyric Poet' (*IIDK* 23),[44] writing in a language she had also engaged with in 'In the Rhine Valley' (*SC* 82). On translating Heine, Cope, who knows some German, says, 'He's difficult to translate without sounding trite.'[45] Her versions maintain the metre, rhyme, and characteristic rhythmical and linguistic lightness of the originals – wherein lies the risk of triteness – occasionally altering syntax to maintain sense, or pulling away slightly in a fillip of reproach or finality entirely characteristic of her more emotive poetry. Thus, in 'Ich glaub nicht an dem Himmel' ('I don't believe in heaven') Heine's final stanza is distinctly different from Cope's. Heine writes:

> Ich glaub nicht an den Bösen,
> An Höll und Höllenschmerz;
> Ich glaub nur an dein Auge,
> Und an dein böses Herz.[46]

Cope renders this as:

> I don't believe in Satan
> Or in the fires of hell.
> Your cold eyes, your indifference –
> They'll do just as well.

Those last two lines of Heine's might more accurately be translated as 'I only believe in your eyes, and in your evil heart' (Heine and Boscombe, 39). Cope has the speaker take unfulfilling, pleading solace in those eyes.

'Cathedral Limerick', written in 1996, is a witty counterpart to her later poems about Christian ceremony in *Family Values* and *Anecdotal Evidence*:

> The choir sings 'Grant us thy salvay-see-oan'
> And I am assailed by temptay-see-oan –
> Seized by the idea
> For this limerick, I fear.
> Lord, grant me improved concentray-see-oan.[47]

The extended words drag out the final feet of the longer lines into paeons, rather than the customary three-syllable anapaests, dactyls, or amphibrachs – with the mournful extra syllable 'oan' emphasising the sense of tedium. Her later poems about church services tend to focus on a love of ritual, but this pokes fun at ritual and suggests the service is a bore – albeit a mildly fruitful one, as it apparently leaves her room to compose the limerick.

Strugnell almost made a surprise return to print in 1999, when Cope wrote 'Jason Strugnell's Royal Wedding Poem', a Shakespearean sonnet composed on the occasion of the wedding of Prince Edward, Earl of Wessex, and Sophie Rhys-Jones. It ends: 'Here's to you both. I hope you like my rhyme. / I will accept a knighthood any time.'[48] This effectively finds Strugnell wanting to be Andrew Motion, whose knighthood in 2009 was virtually nailed on by his appointment as Poet Laureate in the year of the poem's composition. Motion composed his own poem for the wedding as his first Laureate commission, which is as conventional and forgettable as almost any other poem of that derivation, but that contains a timely plea, two years after Diana's death, 'for privacy and what its secrets show'.[49] He also came in for considerable criticism, much of it unfair, at about the time of his appointment (Panecka, 194). Cope knew well what it was like to be derided for being successful, and opted not to publish Strugnell's later effort – perhaps deciding not to pile on, whatever she thought of any attempts to curry Royal favour.

Cope's feelings about the Laureateship bear some superficial affinity with Philip Larkin's: as Motion notes, Larkin had declined the position in 1984, although with some reluctance and with few apparent qualms about the role itself.[50] Cope more closely shares Larkin's agnostic engagement with Anglican liturgy, as hinted at in her decision to translate Heine's 'Ich glaub nicht an dem Himmel', or to write 'Cathedral Limerick', and engaged with more fully in *Family Values* and *Anecdotal Evidence*. The Shakespearean sonnet 'Travel Sonnet', written in 2010 and almost included in *Family Values*,[51] is Larkinesque in a different sense, flatly warning readers to stay put with those they love and not go anywhere. The first twelve lines are taken up with regretting accepting an unspecified 'invitation / To fly so far away all on my own' – the sort of thing Larkin routinely rejected. The poem then ends with an epigrammatic quip implying that in fact no travel is worthwhile, even if you can take loved ones with you: 'You think that you should see the world? Forget it / And just say no next time. You won't regret it.' This is the melodramatic mindset of someone faced imminently with something they do not want to do.

A year later, Cope wrote 'Actaeon's Lover', another Shakespearean sonnet about powerlessness. The poem was commissioned by the National Gallery, who anthologised it,[52] and it is one of the most intriguing poems she has subsequently left out of a book. The best ekphrastic poems tend to explicate a fresh perspective on a painting, rather than simply telling us what we can see for ourselves, and this poem is certainly in that vein. Titian's *Diana and Actaeon* (1556–9) depicts the moment Actaeon sees Diana and the nymphs in the forest, and Cope's speaker is the most obscured of those nymphs, 'the one half hidden by a pillar', who tells of 'My secret love, who loved me too. / [...] That day I couldn't make our rendezvous / Because the Goddess said she needed me'. The poem looks back, as though the speaker is with us, observing the painting as a document of her past, after Actaeon's 'dreadful' death that is in the painting's future, and she mourns in anguish that 'There can be no redress / Against divine Diana, murderess'. Like Cope's earlier ekphrastic poem 'The Sitter' (*IIDK* 20), 'Actaeon's Lover' takes a perspective we might not expect, and is a subversive poem concerned with the fate of an underdog.

In 2018, shortly after the appearance of *Anecdotal Evidence,* Cope published the 94-line *Saint Hilda of Whitby,* in a limited edition of just 100 copies.[53] It is a cantata to mark the 125th anniversary of St Hilda's College, Oxford, set to music by Nicola LeFanu (both artists are alumni), and first performed during the College's celebrations on 18 February 2018. As Cope notes, 'It wasn't quite finished when we put *Anecdotal Evidence* together and, anyway, [Cope's editor at Faber] Matthew Hollis didn't think it fitted.'[54] Certainly it is unique in Cope's oeuvre, taking the form of a short verse play for four characters with interventions from a Chorus, and had it appeared out of context in her most recent collection it might have given the strange impression its author had suddenly and unequivocally found God in an austerely medieval guise. Its principal source is Bede's *Historia Ecclesiastica Gentis Anglorum* (*Ecclesiastical History of the*

English People) (*c.*731), Book IV, Chapters XXIII–XXIV, from which is constructed an imaginative retelling – all of its details lifted from the Latin source – of the story of Saint Hilda (*c.*614–80), Abbess of Whitby Abbey (then known as Streanæshalch). The poem recounts the miracles said to have surrounded her, and principally her influence on the lay brother and cattle-herder Cædmon (*c.*657–84), here 'Caedmon', the earliest named author of an English poem.[55]

The cantata is bookended by the Chorus presenting the same nine simple diegetic lines about Hilda, in which we learn that everyone from royalty to monastic brothers 'Loved the wisdom in her face' and, in a repeated line (so occurring four times in the poem), that 'All who knew her called her mother'. The former quotation is a tightened paraphrase of part of Bede's account;[56] the second is taken verbatim from Bede, who notes, in A. M. Sellar's translation, 'All who knew her called her mother because of her outstanding devotion and grace' (Bede, 329). The poem's first solo speaker is Breguswith, Hilda's mother, who tells how she 'dreamed that my husband was taken away' and that then a 'beautiful necklace of jewels' suddenly appeared on her, and as she reached for them 'a powerful light [...] shone from my hand'. The Chorus then informs us 'The dream came true. And Hilda was that light. / Her father murdered, she in exile learned / Of Christ and of his mysteries'.[57] Events being foreshadowed by dreams becomes a leitmotif in the poem, as do miraculous occurrences surrounding Hilda. She is the poem's unequivocal hero.

We are then told that Bishop Aidan sought her out to become Abbess at Whitby (Cope leaving out Hilda's time in exile from Northumbria and then as a nun at Hartlepool Abbey), and presented with the first of four speeches from Hilda, who decrees that 'all shall live in peace and charity' at Whitby. The Chorus then intervenes to let us know Hilda 'did not think it wrong / To have a banquet, sing a merry song', and here the poem picks up the story of Caedmon, which is given the middle 41 lines, although he only speaks once. Caedmon left the banquet and 'composed himself to rest' (Bede, 333) in the stable – 'To watch the oxen sleeping in the byre', as the poem has it – because he knew no songs so could not join in. While asleep, Bede writes, he dreamed that a voice encouraged him to sing 'the beginning of creation' (Bede, 333). Or, as Caedmon puts it in Cope's poem:

> Reverend Mother, someone stood
> Beside me in my sleep and said
> 'Caedmon, sing to me.' And I
> Replied, 'I cannot sing. That's why
> I left the banquet.' 'Caedmon, sing
> Of God creating everything.'

Although we are told 'All who knew her' did so, Caedmon is the only speaker in the poem to call Hilda 'Mother'. This is a reminder that she is, in a sense, the person who gave metaphorical birth to the person who gave birth to the first extant English poem.

This is then followed by the most remarkable part of Cope's poem, her translation of 'Cædmon's Hymn', his sole remaining work, the discussion of which requires some foregrounding. In *Historia Ecclesiastica,* Bede tells us that 'he straightway began to sing verses to the praise of God the Creator, which he had never heard' (Bede, 333), and then provides a Latin translation of the poem:

> Nunc laudare debemus auctorem regni caelestis,
> potentiam creatoris, et consilium illius
> facta Patris gloriae: quomodo ille,
> cum sit aeternus Deus, omnium miraculorum auctor exstitit;
> qui primo filiis hominum
> caelum pro culmine tecti
> dehinc terram custos humani generis
> omnipotens creavit.[58]

Extant Old English versions of it survive in glosses to and translations of the Latin, such as this eighth-century Northumbrian version:

> Nu scilun herga hefenricæs Uard,
> Metudæs mehti and his modgithanc
> uerc Uuldurfadur, sue he uundra gihuæs,
> eci Dryctin, or astelidæ.
> He ærist scop aeldu barnum
> hefen to hrofæ, halig Sceppend;
> tha middingard moncynnæs Uard,

eci Dryctin, æfter tiadæ
firum foldu, Frea allmehtig.

Elaine Treharne has translated this into modern English, with fidelity to semantics taking necessary precedence over considerations of prosody:

Now we ought to praise the Guardian of the heavenly
  kingdom,
the might of the Creator and his conception,
the work of the glorious Father, as he of each of the wonders,
eternal Lord, established the beginning.
He first created for the sons of men
heaven as a roof, holy Creator;
then the middle-earth, the Guardian of mankind,
the eternal Lord, afterwards made
the earth for men, the Lord almighty.[59]

Bede acknowledges in an aside that 'verses [...] cannot be literally translated out of one language into another without loss of their beauty and loftiness' (Bede, 333). This is a constant challenge for the translator, especially of poetry, and all poetic translations might more accurately be described as 'versions'; although it also provides a creative challenge and opportunity. Cope's version strays from direct translation considerably more than Treharne's. Moreover, it owes more to Bede's rendering than to the Old English, both in lexical choices and the formal decision to avoid the heavy caesurae and alliteration of the original, which typifies Old English verse:

Now let us praise the Maker of heaven,
The mighty Creator and his design.
Let us praise the work of the Father of glory,
The everlasting Lord, Author of all miracles,
The Guardian of the human race,
Who made the sky to be a roof
And then the earth to be our home,
Almighty God.

For the most part, Cope's version retains the four heavy stresses in each line typical of Old English, but does away with them in her especially effusive third and fourth lines, both of which can be stressed either as pentameters or hexameters, and also in the final line, which matches Bede's version by closing with a short sign-off more reminiscent of a prayer. Cope also translates 'Nu scilun herga' ('Now we ought to praise') as the slightly more tentative 'Let us praise', and emphasises this invitation by repeating it in the third line, making Caedmon further stress his already fervent desire to lead collective praise. Moreover, Cope omits the reference to 'middingard', 'middle-earth', the world inhabited by humans in a medieval Germanic conception of cosmology, keeping the more readily understood 'earth', and avoids the linguistic omission of women from God's Creation. In doing so, Cope also plays with the order of the original: her fifth line is a version of the second half of the seventh in the original, and her sixth line is a version of the original fifth and first half of the sixth, with the two half-lines between omitted. As a result, her rendering simplifies the construction of the original in its fifth to seventh lines, so that we are presented with God the protector who made the heavens and then the earth, and it contains one fewer line than the original and other verse translations: she has, uniquely among published versions, abridged this nine-line poem in her translation, as well as simplifying it.

Saint Hilda then goes on to abridge Bede's account of what happened next: Hilda tells Caedmon, 'You are indeed inspired by heavenly grace', and 'Henceforward Caedmon spent his cloistered days / Learning Holy Scripture' and writing 'songs of praise'.[60] Then we learn that he 'died a peaceful death;[61] on the other hand, 'Begu (a nun)' informs us in the poem's final solo passage that Hilda endured 'years of suffering'. The nun then recounts that she, too, had a premonitory dream: 'Of Hilda's soul ascending'. Then 'after I awoke at break of day / They brought me news that she had passed away'. Bede writes that Begu was a nun at Hacanos (Hackness), thirteen miles from Whitby (Bede, 334), although Cope's poem leaves it implied that she is in a different part of the same monastery, directly under Hilda's care.[62] Here, in any case, Begu's account mirrors Caedmon's miracle, precipitated by a somnambulant revelation. Hilda's life is thus marked both at its inception and end by miracles, further implying that Caedmon's miracle in the middle of her life was also a product of Hilda's divinity.

Cope's poem is accessible to a wide modern audience; many academic accounts are not, and of course neither are the Latin and Old English originals. Her poem embraces the didactic tone common to Old English verse, but uses this both to give it an austerely medieval air and to concentrate the complex narrative into an easily digestible, relatively short, highly readable piece. She also makes other minor adjustments that might irritate scholars, but aid wider comprehension. For example, she eschews Old English spellings that often used letters and other scriptural elements not familiar now (for example, Breguswīþ becomes Breguswith); Streonæshalch is not mentioned and is replaced with the familiar Whitby, a place name resulting from Viking invasion postdating Hilda's time; and her poem's speeches, with the exception of 'Cædmon's Hymn', almost entirely ring with the inherent musicality of more modern rhymed pentameters or tetramaters. Moreover, the poem is noteworthy for emphasising that the herder-poet's 'miracle', and therefore the symbolic birth of the English poetic tradition, was the result of the miraculous effects of Saint Hilda. It highlights a woman's role that has largely been overshadowed in cultural memory, and gives that to us in fresh, simple language.

In June 2019, Cope stated that she had written almost nothing since *Saint Hilda of Whitby*, and claimed that 'my work [as a poet] may be finished'.[63] Her most recent poem at that time, 'Obit', completed in December 2018, is a return to the familiar territory of the villanelle. It begins with an epigraph from an obituary in *The Times*, which is then used for one of the repetends: 'He never knowingly cracked a joke'. The subject can be none other than the British civil servant Lord Jeremy Heywood of Whitehall, who died on 4 November 2018, and served under the Labour governments of Blair and Brown, and the Conservative governments of Cameron and May, most recently as Cabinet Secretary (2012–18).[64] He is not named in the poem, however, and really the human subject could be any of a multitude of bureaucrats:

> Yesterday the world awoke
> To mourn the news that he had died –
> This first-rate sober-sided bloke,
> Who never knowingly cracked a joke.[65]

Even this po-faced respectful account contains an Easter egg for anyone who looks up the source of the epigraph and repeated line, for in the obituary he is described in the opening paragraph as 'the most powerful man in Britain that most people have never heard of'. In other words, it didn't. This poem was followed in autumn 2019 by two triolets – one called 'Old Ladies', which ends: 'we're old ladies with our sticks, / Who once, perhaps, were hot.'[66] The last line reads as though a scandalous lecher is passing judgement, rather than the speaker – perhaps Prime Minister Boris Johnson, in fact, who inspired the other triolet, 'Girly Swot'. That is the term Johnson used to refer to his fellow Old Etonian, former Prime Minister David Cameron, in a cabinet paper – and as an insult by feminisation it was bound to get Cope's back up.[67] Her rejoinder is a poem in praise of being both 'girl' and 'swot', the implication being that Johnson might fare better if he boned up a bit himself and didn't so readily embrace an aggressive masculinity.[68] Cope may have slowed down insofar as writing poems is concerned, but she has not lost any sharpness.

At the time of writing, in 2020, these few quips in repeating forms are her last poems, and she has 'not felt like writing a poem since'.[69] Hers can be regarded as a remarkable, often witty, often pained, frequently witty and pained, highly readable, modestly proportioned, stubbornly unfashionable body of work – more varied, intelligent, and allusive than is typically supposed, as I hope to have demonstrated. However, the potential beginnings of a sixth collection exist, and Cope has never been a poet to rush her art.

Notes

INTRODUCTION

1. 'Wendy Cope: I Don't Want to be Laureate', *The Guardian* (2 June 2008) <www.theguardian.com/books/2008/jun/02/hayfestival2008.guardianhayfestival> [accessed 23 August 2019].
2. From a private letter, 1992.
3. Wendy Cope archive, British Library, at MS89108/1/14.
4. Wendy Cope archive, British Library, at MS89108/1/14.
5. Gerry Cambridge, 'Poetic Assessment: Wendy Cope', *Acumen*, 26 (1996), 46–9, at 48.
6. Rowan Williams, 'A Tour of the Archive with Dr Rowan Williams', Poetry Archive website <poetryarchive.org/guided-tour/tour-archive-dr-rowan-williams> [accessed 5 April 2019].
7. The former is, of course, dead, his oeuvre complete; the latter is effectively known only as a parodist. The book contains work by more than 150 writers. All of Cope's parodies are taken from her first collection – the largest haul in the anthology from a single-authored volume. John Gross, ed., *The Oxford Book of Parodies* (Oxford: Oxford University Press, 2010).
8. A. M. Juster, '"Anecdotal Evidence" in the Case of Wendy Cope', *Los Angeles Review of Books* (27 February 2018) < lareviewofbooks.org/article/anecdotal-evidence-in-the-case-of-wendy-cope/> [accessed 1 April 2019].
9. Julie Kane, 'Mortality and Mellowing: On Wendy Cope', *The Dark Horse*, 27 (2011), 90–5, at 91–2.
10. Ian Gregson, *Contemporary Poetry and Postmodernism: Dialogue and Estrangement* (Basingstoke: Macmillan, 1998), 4–5.
11. Henry King, 'Memorable Speech', *PN Review*, 184 (2008), 79–80, at 80.
12. Rebecca Watts, 'Facts and Verdicts', *PN Review*, 219 (2014), 66–7, at 67.

13. Richard O'Brien, *The Spectator* (25 October 1986). Admittedly, it is not easy to make sense of the notion that wit is a limitation. Cope quoted this as the epigraph to 'Serious Concerns' (*SC* 15). Cope is also largely ignored by feminist critics; for example, she receives no mention in Vicki Bertram, *Gendering Poetry: Contemporary Poetry and Sexual Politics* (London: Rivers Oram, 2005).
14. Michael Schmidt, *Lives of the Poets* (London: Phoenix, 1998), 863.
15. William Logan, 'A Letter from Britain (Part II)', *Poetry*, 157.5 (1992), 290–9, at 293.
16. Nicola Thompson, 'Wendy Cope's Struggle with Strugnell in *Making Cocoa for Kingsley Amis*', *New Perspectives on Women and Comedy*, ed. Regina Barreca (Philadelphia, PA, USA: Gordon and Breach, 1992), 111–22, at 116.
17. Anthony Thwaite, *Poetry Today: A Critical Guide to British Poetry 1960–95* (London: Routledge, 1996), 127–8.

CHAPTER 1: 'I LEARNED TO GET MY OWN BACK': *MAKING COCOA FOR KINGSLEY AMIS* (1986)

1. Anthony Thwaite, *Poetry Today: A Critical Guide to British Poetry 1960–95* (London: Routledge, 1996), 127.
2. *Desert Island Discs*, BBC Radio 4 (1 February 2019).
3. Robert Fulford, 'Laughing at Dreary Old Poets: Wendy Cope is First Fresh Voice in English Poetry for Years', *Toronto Star* (30 August 1986), M6.
4. More than 180,000 by 2018, according to The Poetry Archive <poetryarchive.org> [accessed 22 June 2019].
5. Peter Riley, 'Making Money', *PN Review*, 13.1 (1986), 79.
6. According to Cope's own notes on the poem. Wendy Cope, 'Wendy Cope: Making Cocoa for Kingsley Amis', *The Guardian* (18 May 2013) <theguardian.com/books/interactive/2013/may/18/wendy-cope-making-cocoa-kingsley-annotations> [accessed 11 June 2019]
7. Tony Harrison, *Laureate's Block and Other Poems* (London: Penguin, 2000), 12. The poem of Motion's to which Harrison alludes is 'Mythology' (1997), an elegy for Princess Diana, in which 'swerving underground, / the future tracked you, snapping at your heels: / Diana, breathless, hunted by your own quick hounds' (Andrew Motion, *Public Property* (London: Faber, 2003), 55). When Motion's decade-long tenure as Laureate was drawing to an end, Cope made her feelings on the Laureateship known: 'it is an archaic post and means nothing'. 'Female Contenders Rule Out "Archaic" Post of Poet Laureate', *The Independent* (10 June 2008) <independent.co.uk/arts-entertainment/books/news/

female-contenders-rule-out-archaic-post-of-poet-laureate-843537.html> [accessed 22 June 2019].

8. A. Alvarez, 'Ted Hughes', *The Epic Poise: A Celebration of Ted Hughes*, ed. Nick Gammage (London: Faber & Faber, 1999), 207–11, at 210.
9. Richard Collins and James Purnell, 'Introduction', *Reservoirs of Dogma*, ed. Richard Collins and James Purnell (London: Institute for Public Policy Research, 1996), 1–9, at 3.
10. Louise Tondeur, 'Risk, Constraint, Play: A New Paradigm for Examining Practice-research in the Academy', *Text Journal*, 21.1 (2017) <textjournal.com.au/april17/tondeur.htm> [accessed 4 June 2019].
11. See, for example, Wendy Cope, 'Ageing' (2011) (*LLA* 171–5, at 172). Such children's books are often referred to as 'Peter and Jane books', after their two main characters.
12. <im-possible.info/english/art/delprete> [accessed 15 June 2019].
13. 'Libra is the sign of partnerships and relationships […]. Libra feels weak on its own.' Joanna Martine Woolfolk, *Libra* (Plymouth: Taylor Trade Publishing, 2011), 3.
14. Philip Larkin, *The Complete Poems*, ed. Archie Burnett (London: Faber, 2012), 61.
15. Geoffrey Chaucer, *The Riverside Chaucer*, ed. Larry D. Benson and F. N. Robinson (Oxford: Oxford University Press, 1987), 154–68.
16. Charles Causley, *Collected Poems: 1951–2000* (London: Picador, 2000), 421.
17. William Wordsworth, *The Prelude*, v, lines 389–90, *The Collected Poems of William Wordsworth* (Ware: Wordsworth Editions, 1994), 671.
18. Andrew Bennett, 'Romantic Poets and Contemporary Poetry', *The Cambridge Companion to British Romantic Poetry*, ed. James Chandler and Maureen N. McLane (Cambridge: Cambridge University Press, 2008), 263–78, at 270.
19. In earlier drafts, she had instead written 'And he replied', before settling on the comically leaden archaism – also changing 'joyful bleat' to 'jocund bleat', with similar effects. Wendy Cope archive, British Library, at MS89108/1/96.
20. William Wordsworth and Samuel Taylor Coleridge, *Lyrical Ballads* (1800), ed. R. L. Brett and A. R. Jones (London: Routledge, 2005), 204.
21. William Kerr, 'Counting Sheep', *Georgian Poetry V*, ed. Edward Marsh (London: Poetry Bookshop, 1922), 112.
22. Marta Pérez Novales, 'Wendy Cope's Use of Parody in *Making Cocoa for Kingsley Amis*', *Miscelánea: A Journal of English and American Studies*, 15 (1994), 481–500, at 488.
23. William Logan, 'A Letter from Britain (Part II)', *Poetry*, 157.5 (1992), 290–9, at 293.

24. T. S. Eliot, *The Waste Land and Other Poems* (London: Faber, 1999), 32–3.
25. D. M. Thomas encouraged Cope on this point, writing 'there can be Strugnell poems without Strugnell; as there are *Crow* poems [by Ted Hughes] without Crow'. Wendy Cope archive, British Library, at MS89108/1/17.
26. Nicola Thompson, 'Wendy Cope's Struggle with Strugnell in *Making Cocoa for Kingsley Amis*', *New Perspectives on Women and Comedy*, ed. Regina Barreca (Philadelphia, PA, USA: Gordon and Breach, 1992), 111–22, at 116.
27. Alongside T. S. Eliot. John Shakespeare, 'Larkin's First Interview: How Philip Larkin Rewrote the First, Indiscreet Article About Him to Appear in the British Press', *The Times Literary Supplement* (1 April 2009), 12. Cope epitomises Betjeman as 'celebrating a kind of suburban life that's a horror to me'. Wendy Cope and William Baer, 'Wendy Cope', William Baer, *Fourteen on Form: Conversations with Poets* (Jackson, MS, USA: University Press of Mississippi, 2004), 153–71, at 167.
28. Ted Hughes, *Crow* (London: Faber, 1972), 22.
29. Henry King, 'Memorable Speech', *PN Review*, 35.2 (2008), 79–80, at 80.
30. Wendy Cope, 'Ted Hughes in the Classroom' (1999) (*LLA* 79–81).
31. Wendy Cope, 'It's a Free Country' (2008), (*LLA* 145–6, at 145).
32. Wendy Cope, 'Larkin's "First Sight"' (2001) (*LLA* 217–18, at 217).
33. This admiration is evident in several letters held in the Wendy Cope archive, British Library, at MS89108/1/14. According to Cope, Raine also suggested that the title poem of her first collection should have its own section at the back of the book and, in fact, be made the title poem. <theguardian.com/books/interactive/2013/may/18/wendy-cope-making-cocoa-kingsley-annotations> [accessed 11 June 2018]. She has given him 'special thanks for believing in my ability to write'. 'Introduction', *LLA* 1–3, at 3.
34. Craig Raine, *The Onion, Memory* (Oxford: Oxford University Press, 1978), 2–8.
35. Adrian Henri, *Collected Poems: 1967–85* (London: Allison and Busby, 1986), 105.
36. Lulu Morris, 'Cereal Masturbation', *National Geographic* (2018) <nationalgeographic.com.au/history/cereal-masturbation.aspx> [accessed: 9 October 2019].
37. The poem bears a long dedication in which Strugnell claims to have been 'influenced' by a host of 'great men' such as Marcel Proust and Allen Ginsberg – although he leaves out the one poet his poem rips off, as though he would like to hide that while simultaneously hoping for glory by vague association with the others.
38. Seamus Heaney, *North* (London: Faber, 1975).

39. For example, Philip Sidney's *Astrophel and Stella* (1591) contains 108 sonnets, Edmund Spenser's *Amoretti* (1594) 88, and Shakespeare's *Sonnets* (1609) 154.
40. Timothy Steele, 'Verse Satire in the Twentieth Century', *A Companion to Satire,* ed. Ruben Qunitero (Malden, MA, USA: Blackwell, 2007), 434–59, at 441.
41. William Shakespeare, *Shakespeare's Sonnets,* ed. Katherine Duncan-Jones (London: Arden, 2010), 369.
42. U. A. Fanthorpe, *Selected Poems* (London: Penguin, 1986), 28–9.
43. István D. Rácz, 'Heaneys of the Mind', *Hungarian Journal of English and American Studies,* 10.1/2 (2004), 127–36, at 135.
44. *The Penguin Book of Contemporary British Poetry,* ed. Andrew Motion and Blake Morrison (London: Penguin, 1982). Morrison had led a poetry criticism group attended by Cope in the late 1970s.
45. Of the 21 poets in that book, 16 are men – largely reflective of the gender split in British poetry publishing at the time, but also a reminder that Cope was entering a predominantly male poetry world. Heaney is the first poet in the book, which might surprise anyone who knows how British he felt. In 'An Open Letter', first published in 1983, he writes: 'My passport's green. / No glass of ours was ever raised / To toast The Queen'. Seamus Heaney, *An Open Letter* (Dublin: Field Day, 1983).
46. Previously unpublished 'Strugnell sonnets' are discussed in the final chapter.
47. Christopher Reid, 'Here Comes Amy', *London Review of Books,* 8.7 (1986), 20–2, at 22. Reid would take over from Raine as Cope's editor at Faber before the publication of her second collection.
48. Kingsley Amis, *Collected Poems: 1944–1979* (New York, NY, USA: New York Review of Books, 2016), 56.
49. Although the collection also contains a specific dedication 'to Arthur S. Couch and everyone who helped'. The appropriately named Couch was her therapist. 'Everyone else' must surely include the men parodied in the book.

CHAPTER 2: 'HE THINKS YOU'RE CRAZY': *SERIOUS CONCERNS* (1992)

1. Christina Patterson, 'Behold, A Happy Poet' (interview), *The Independent* (30 May 2008) <independent.co.uk/arts-entertainment/books/features/behold-a-happy-poet-836309.html> [accessed 12 June 2019].
2. Thomas Sutcliffe, 'Wendy Cope: The Unromantic Poet of Love', *The Independent* (7 June 2001) <independent.co.uk/news/people/profiles/

wendy-cope-the-unromantic-poet-of-love-5364449.html> [accessed 21 January 2019].

3. Julie Kane, 'Mortality and Mellowing: On Wendy Cope', *The Dark Horse*, 27 (2011), 90–5, at 94.
4. *Desert Island Discs*, BBC Radio 4 (1 February 2019).
5. Lucinda Everett, 'Wendy Cope: "My editor says she'd die of shock if she saw me on Twitter"', *The Telegraph* (21 November 2014) <telegraph.co.uk/culture/books/authorinterviews/11238664/Wendy-Cope-My-editor-says-shed-die-of-shock-if-she-saw-me-on-Twitter.html> [accessed 19 February 2019].
6. In the 1990s, this poem came 50th in the BBC's hunt to find Britain's favourite poem, ahead of all but two of her living contemporaries (Jenny Joseph and Allan Ahlberg). *The Nation's Favourite Poem* (London: BBC, 1996), 80.
7. Cope notes that 'the idea of the buses all showing up at once isn't limited to one sex', and the poem 'could've just as easily have been titled "Bloody Women"', although 'it would be a lot more difficult [...] for a man to write with the same freedom and honesty about his ambivalence towards women'. Wendy Cope and William Baer, 'Wendy Cope', William Baer, *Fourteen on Form: Conversations with Poets* (Jackson, MS, USA: University Press of Mississippi, 2004), 153–71, at 157.
8. Intriguingly, her then-nascent relationship with Lachlan Mackinnon was the motivation for 'Flowers', the last poem written for inclusion in *Serious Concerns*. However, Cope opted to keep its inspiration hidden and fold the poem in among ones of romantic dissatisfaction. Conversation with author, 8 August 2019.
9. Thomas Hardy, *The Collected Poems of Thomas Hardy*, ed. Michael Irwin (Ware: Wordsworth Editions, 1994), 150.
10. Cope had recently published *Twiddling Your Thumbs: Hand Rhymes*, a collection of poems for children with accompanying illustrated hand gestures. It perhaps goes without saying that none of these were concerned with seeing a therapist – or, as is the second of the 'Two Hand Rhymes for Grown-ups', with publishers.
11. Robert D. Stolorow, 'Toward a Functional Definition of Narcissism', *Essential Papers on Narcissism*, ed. Andrew P. Morrison (New York, NY, USA: New York University Press, 1986), 197–210, at 203.
12. Cope's notebooks from the 1980s include many less helpless unfinished poems about therapy, implying that the impression she gives about it in her published poems is only part of her truth. Wendy Cope archive, British Library, at MS89108/1/55.
13. For example, the same form had recently been used throughout Roald Dahl's immensely popular *Revolting Rhymes* (London:

Jonathan Cape, 1982), *Dirty Beasts* (London: Jonathan Cape, 1983), and *Rhyme Stew* (London: Jonathan Cape, 1989).

14. Mark Oakley, *The Collage of God* (Norwich: Canterbury Press, 2001), 89. Oakley is consciously paraphrasing William Hazlitt.
15. Philip Larkin, *The Complete Poems,* ed. Archie Burnett (London: Faber, 2012), 88.
16. This poem echoes Shakespeare's 'Sonnet 130'. William Shakespeare, *Shakespeare's Sonnets,* ed. Katherine Duncan-Jones (London: Arden, 2010), 371.
17. Stephen Regan, *The Sonnet* (Oxford: Oxford University Press, 2019), 374.
18. W. B. Yeats, *Selected Poems,* ed. Timothy Webb (London: Penguin, 2000), 124.
19. Marta Pérez Novales, 'Wendy Cope's Use of Parody in *Making Cocoa for Kingsley Amis*', *Miscelánea: A Journal of English and American Studies,* 15 (1994), 481–500, at 483.
20. Such matters were central to the United Nations Conference on Environment and Development (UNCED) (the 'Earth Summit') in Rio de Janeiro, 1992.
21. While book-length studies of poetry and ecology existed before 1992, such as John Elder, *Imagining the Earth: Poetry and the Vision of Nature* (Chicago, IL, USA: University of Illinois Press, 1985), the first texts to use the term 'ecopoetry', such as J. Scott Bryson, ed., *Ecopoetry: A Critical Introduction* (Salt Lake City, UT, USA: Utah University Press, 2002), did not appear until long after *Serious Concerns.*
22. The 'concerned adolescent' speaker's disproportionate belief in the importance of his or her writing is not only a youthful curse, and will be familiar to almost anyone who knows enough poets.
23. The ordination of women priests in the Church of England would begin in 1994, and was a topical matter in the preceding years.
24. Heathcoat Williams, *Whale Nation* (London: Cape, 1988).
25. Cope claims no meaning behind the name change, so the second of these is apparently a happy accident. 'My parents worked together in the same business [and often mentioned] an accountant called Pagnell. I think that's why "Strugnell" appealed when I looked through a telephone directory for a name for my poet. [...] I've sometimes felt guilty about real people called Strugnell, especially if they want to be published writers. [...] Strugnell's first appearance was an entry in a *New Statesman* competition. [...] I think it was something to do with the Rubaiyat [so I called him] Omar. When Strugnell wrote more I called him Jason – not sure why. He sometimes changed it to Jake.' (Email correspondence with author,

23 July 2019.) As seen in chapter seven, Jason was indeed used before (and after) Jake, although only the latter appears in her debut.

26. Jerome Rothenberg, *Technicians of the Sacred: A Range of Poetries from Africa, America, Asia, Europe and Oceania* (3rd edn) (Oakland, CA, USA: University of California Press, 2017).
27. See, for example, Julian Cowley, 'Performing the Wor(l)d: Contemporary British Concrete Poetry', *In Black and Gold: Contiguous Traditions in Post-War British and Irish Poetry*, ed. C. C. Barfoot (Amsterdam, Netherlands: Rodopi, 1994), 179–98, at 184.
28. *The Verb*, BBC Radio 3 (14 October 2016). One later Strugnell poem exists: 'Jason Strugnell's Royal Wedding Poem' (1999). See chapter seven.
29. William Carlos Williams, *Selected Poems* (London: Penguin, 2000), 57.
30. Geoffrey Chaucer, *The Riverside Chaucer*, ed. Larry D. Benson and F. N. Robinson (Oxford: Oxford University Press, 1987), 394, lines 675–90.

CHAPTER 3: 'STILL WARM, STILL WARM': *IF I DON'T KNOW* (2001)

1. Nicola Thompson, 'Wendy Cope's Struggle with Strugnell in *Making Cocoa for Kingsley Amis*', *New Perspectives on Women and Comedy*, ed. Regina Barreca (Philadelphia, PA, USA: Gordon and Breach, 1992), 111–22, at 122.
2. Wendy Cope and William Baer, 'Wendy Cope', William Baer, *Fourteen on Form: Conversations with Poets* (Jackson, MS, USA: University Press of Mississippi, 2004), 153–71, at 168.
3. Christina Patterson, '*Family Values* by Wendy Cope', *The Independent* (11 April 2011) <independent.co.uk/arts-entertainment/books/reviews/family-values-by-wendy-cope-2264676.html> [accessed 15 February 2019].
4. Kate Kellaway, 'Of Headless Squirrels and Men', *The Guardian* (3 June 2001) <amp.theguardian.com/books/2001/jun/03/poetry.features2> [accessed 20 February 2019].
5. Wendy Cope and Rivka Isaacson, 'Wendy Cope Interview: "You know, there's some sadness in me"' (interview), *The Independent* (8 November 2014) <independent.co.uk/arts-entertainment/books/features/poet-wendy-cope-interview-you-know-there-s-some-sadness-in-me-9847592.html> [accessed 15 February 2019].
6. Bob Holmes, 'Why Time Flies in Old Age', *New Scientist* (23 November 1996) <newscientist.com/article/mg15220571-700-why-time-flies-in-old-age/> [accessed 15 February 2019].

7. Henry King, 'Memorable Speech', *PN Review*, 35.2 (2008), 79–80, at 80.
8. *The River Wey* <weyriver.co.uk/theriver/getknow.htm> [accessed 18 February 2019].
9. The river has since largely recovered. However, and perhaps inevitably, there have been subsequent pollutions, including oil and sewage spillages. See, for example, Jenny Stanton, '"Sewage" Pollution Kills Fish and Eels in River Wey Tributary', *Surrey Live* (1 July 2014) <getsurrey.co.uk/news/surrey-news/chiddingold-sewage-pollution-investigated-environment-7347728> [accessed 18 February 2018].
10. Helen Lewis, 'Wendy Cope: "I can't die until I've sorted out the filing cabinets"', *New Statesman* (3 December 2011) <newstatesman.com/blogs/helen-lewis-hasteley/2011/11/cope-poems-british-poets#amp> [accessed 19 February 2019].
11. Interview with Ian McMillan, *The Verb*, BBC Radio 3 (14 October 2016).
12. Wendy Cope and Sam Leith, 'Books Podcast: Wendy Cope' (podcast), *The Spectator* (2018) <blogs.spectator.co.uk/2018/03/books-podcast-wendy-cope/> [accessed 12 March 2019].
13. Judith Collins and Elsbeth Lindner, ed., *Writing on the Wall: Women Writers on Women Artists* (London: Weidenfeld & Nicolson, 1993).
14. William Shakespeare, *Shakespeare's Sonnets*, ed. Katherine Duncan-Jones (London: Arden, 2010), 147.
15. A draft of this, in which a crossed-out potential penultimate stanza includes the words 'no poet can resist a corpse', makes explicit what the finished poem leaves implicit. Wendy Cope archive, British Library, at MS89108/1/114.
16. Edwin Morgan, *Collected Poems* (Manchester: Carcanet, 1990), 132–6.
17. Heinrich Heine, *Selected Verse*, trans. Peter Boscombe (London: Penguin, 1968), 19. Cope has translated some of Heine's poems. See chapter seven.
18. In her acknowledgements for the collection, Cope thanks 'the Hawthornden Castle International Retreat for Writers, where I stayed for a month in 1993 and wrote four poems'.
19. John Berryman, *The Dream Songs* (New York: Farrar, Straus and Giroux, 1969). This book combines two previous works, the earlier of which, *77 Dream Songs* (New York: Farrar, Straus and Giroux, 1964), also doesn't include the definite article. It is possible, although not probable since the later volume had effectively succeeded it, that this is the book Cope's speaker is reading.
20. This haul also included two unpublished 'Dream Songs' – one discernibly weaker, the other too focused on the characteristics of her cohort at the retreat to have wider resonance. Wendy Cope archive, British Library, at MS89108/1/114.

21. Thomas Sutcliffe, 'Wendy Cope: The Unromantic Poet of Love', *The Independent* (7 June 2001) <independent.co.uk/news/people/profiles/wendy-cope-the-unromantic-poet-of-love-5364449.html> [accessed 23 June 2019].
22. This poem is discussed in chapter six.
23. Wendy Cope archive, British Library, at MS89108/1/122.
24. Charles Causley, *Collected Poems* (London: Picador, 2000), 65.

CHAPTER 4: 'YOUR ANGER IS A SIN': *FAMILY VALUES* (2011)

1. Helen Lewis, 'Wendy Cope: "I can't die until I've sorted out the filing cabinets"', *New Statesman* (3 December 2011) <newstatesman.com/blogs/helen-lewis-hasteley/2011/11/cope-poems-british-poets#amp> [accessed 19 February 2019].
2. *Desert Island Discs*, BBC Radio 4 (1 February 2019).
3. Most of Cope's Christmas poems are collected in Wendy Cope, *Christmas Poems* (London: Faber, 2017), which includes two poems from *Serious Concerns*, one from *If I Don't Know*, four from *Family Values*, and two that would soon appear in her fifth collection, *Anecdotal Evidence*, alongside three previously uncollected poems.
4. Wendy Cope, 'Foreword', Mark Oakley, *The Collage of God* (Norwich: Canterbury Press, 2001), ix–x.
5. Tom Payne, 'A Page in the Life: Wendy Cope', *The Telegraph* (28 March 2011) <telegraph.co.uk/culture/books/bookreviews/8404207/A-Page-in-the-Life-Wendy-Cope.html> [accessed 8 March 2019].
6. This poem went viral on social media when Donald Trump became President of the United States in 2016, some assuming it had been written to mark the occasion.
7. Several drafts are in the third person, Cope evidently hitting upon the strength of using the more unusual second person in the course of composition. Moreover, in draft, 'All this has been ordained by God' was 'The bad incur the wrath of God'. Again, the change forces checkmate, here through the imposition of faulty logic: if the fallacy is taken as ordination, we cannot argue with it, whereas 'badness' is subjective. Wendy Cope archive, British Library, at MS89108/1/114.
8. Cope has said of her mother, 'She didn't actually believe the earth was flat [but] she did believe the world began with Adam and Eve' (Payne). The implication is that the second belief is as ludicrously unscientific as the first.

9. Mackinnon might have had in mind poems by Larkin such as 'Aubade', in which death is 'a standing chill / That slows each impulse down to indecision', or 'Dockery and Son', in which 'Life is first boredom, then fear'. Philip Larkin, *The Complete Poems*, ed. Archie Burnett (London: Faber, 2012), 116 and 66, respectively. Wendy Cope archive, British Library, at MS89108/1/90 and MS89108/1/122.
10. Kate Kellaway, '*Family Values* by Wendy Cope', *The Guardian* (15 May 2011) <theguardian.com/books/2011/may/15/family-values-wendy-cope-poetry> [accessed 8 March 2019].
11. Margaret Ferguson, Mary Jo Salter, and Jon Stallworthy, ed., *The Norton Anthology of Poetry* (5th edn) (New York, NY, USA: Norton, 2005), 16.
12. Alun Lewis, *Collected Poems*, ed. Cary Archard (Bridgend: Seren, 1994), 29.
13. Sophie Hannah, 'Between Heart and Head', *PN Review*, 200 (2011), 76–7, at 76.
14. Carol Ann Duffy, *Collected Poems* (London: Picador, 2015), 226.
15. The sequence's title implies that other audience members are not presented, although three others nearly were: 'The Drinker', 'The Appreciative Listener', and 'The Amateur Conductor', a counterpart to 'The Cougher' (whose difficulty was perhaps deemed too similar), whose 'foot is on the move again / And now my hand is joining in'. Wendy Cope archive, British Library, at MS89108/1/89.

CHAPTER 5: 'ABOUT THE HUMAN HEART': *ANECDOTAL EVIDENCE* (2018)

1. Cope's private archive, Ely.
2. See, for example, Bill Bradfield, ed., *Books and Reading: A Book of Quotations* (Mineola, NY, USA: Dover, 2012), 30.
3. See, for example, Florence Hardy, *The Life of Thomas Hardy* (London: Macmillan, 1962), 171.
4. In draft, the first of these lines was 'It feels as if I'll be cast adrift'. The final version is more uncompromising. 2011–12 notebook, Cope's private archive, Ely.
5. Philip Larkin, *The Complete Poems*, ed. Archie Burnett (London: Faber, 2012), 118.
6. Before the seventeenth-century draining of the Fens, Ely was an island in the marshes. Intriguingly, the second abbey at what was to become Ely was dedicated in the tenth century to St Æthelthryth by Æthelwold of Winchester, the city Cope and Mackinnon had left in 2011, although this is not alluded to in the poem.

7. Cope's private archive, Ely.
8. William Shakespeare, *Shakespeare's Sonnets*, ed. Katherine Duncan-Jones (London: Arden, 2010), 147.
9. Tony Harrison, *Collected Poems* (London: Viking, 2007), 138.
10. Cope's only previous 'serious' haiku poem in her adult collections is 'Elegy for the Northern Wey' (*IIDK* 51), which is also about a river, although that is hardly a poem of contentment.
11. The author is unable to find an article from *The Daily Telegraph* with that headline. The previous day, the following article was published: Matthew Day, 'Wanted: One Pied Piper – Hamelin Suffering from Rat Problem Again', *The Daily Telegraph* (24 May 2012). It tells a very similar story to the poem. <telegraph.co.uk/news/worldnews/europe/germany/9287658/Wanted-one-Pied-Piper-Hamelin-suffering-from-rat-problem-again.html> [accessed 1 April 2019].
12. A. M. Juster, '"Anecdotal Evidence" in the Case of Wendy Cope', *Los Angeles Review of Books* (27 February 2018) <lareviewofbooks.org/article/anecdotal-evidence-in-the-case-of-wendy-cope/> [accessed 1 April 2019].
13. Cope is alluding to 'I Am the Very Model of a Modern Major-General', a patter song from Gilbert and Sullivan's *The Pirates of Penzance* (1879), in which the narrating General sings in a clipped upper-class accent that neatly serves to hide the forced rhyme. Cope had made similar structural use of another song from this opera in 'A Policeman's Lot' (*MC* 5), discussed in chapter one.
14. *Desert Island Discs*, BBC Radio 4 (1 February 2019).
15. 'A Wreath for George Herbert' laments that 'I can't share your faith' (*AE* 42), and in 'A Poem about Jesus' – to date, her last poetic comment on faith – she reverts to agnosticism to write, 'I don't know if he rose from the grave' (*AE* 43). Note the added doubt in the decision not to capitalise the first letter of the pronoun. While it is dangerous to conflate a speaker with an author, Cope's poetic voice is largely consistent unless she is obviously adopting a parodic persona.
16. Jay Livingston and Ray Evans, 'Que Sera, Sera' (Whatever Will Be, Will Be)', sung by Doris Day in the Alfred Hitchcock film *The Man Who Knew Too Much* (1956).
17. 'Men Talking', written in June 2010, was the earliest. Wendy Cope, 2009–11 notebook, in Cope's private archive, Ely.

CHAPTER 6: 'THE GIFT OF CHANGING': COPE'S POEMS FOR CHILDREN

1. Wendy Cope, 'Wendy Cope', *The Artist in Time: A Generation of Great British Creatives,* ed. Chris Fite-Wassilak (London: Herbert Press, 2020), 34–41, at 34.
2. This is the pedagogical method of helping learners to build understanding by encouraging them into new territory they can negotiate with support. See, for example, Seth Chaiklin, 'The Zone of Proximal Development in Vygotsky's Analysis of Learning and Instruction', *Vygotsky's Educational Theory in Cultural Context,* ed. Alex Kozulin, Boris Gindis, Vladimir S. Ageyev, and Suzanne M. Miller (Cambridge: Cambridge University Press, 2003), 39–64.
3. Collins Big Cat website <collins.co.uk/pages/collins-big-cat> [accessed 23 April 2019].
4. This haiku dates from a spate of haiku-writing in 1973, long before Cope started publishing, and was not apparently initially written for children. It is one of the earliest written of her poems to be published, and it demonstrates the longevity of her continued interest in haiku. Wendy Cope archive, British Library, at MS89108/1/90.
5. See, for example, Roger McGough, ed., *100 Best Poems for Children* (London: Penguin, 2002). The poem was written 'in the early 1980s' (email correspondence with author, 23 June 2019).
6. The others are 'Kate', about a girl 'who became obsessed with a puzzle and went mad', which remains unpublished, and 'Stephen', about a boy who died for want of a working television, which won the Humberside Children's Poetry Competition 1984. Wendy Cope archive, British Library, at MS89108/1/88. The latter was later published in Wes Magee, ed., *Cambridge Contemporary Poets 2* (Cambridge: Cambridge University Press, 1992), 84–5. Magee had judged the competition.
7. *Humour in Verse: An Anthology,* ed. W. E. Slater (Cambridge: Cambridge University Press, 1959), 91–2. In this and the other tales in Hilaire Belloc, *Cautionary Tales for Children* (London: Eveleigh Nash, 1907), Belloc was parodying more sententious cautionary tales for children from the previous century.
8. Cope has said, 'I think it is suitable for people of about twelve and over' (email correspondence with author, 5 April 2019).
9. Tony Harrison, *Collected Poems* (London: Viking, 2007), 263–79.
10. T. S. Eliot, *The Waste Land and Other Poems* (London: Faber, 1999), 30. Edmund Spenser, 'Prothalamion', Edmund Spenser, *The Shorter Poems,* ed. Richard McCabe (London: Penguin, 1999), 491–8. Spenser's poem repeats the line 'Sweet Thames, run softly, till I end my song' as the last of each of its eighteen-line stanzas.

11. In 'Defining the Problem', published a year after *The River Girl*, she crystallises this into an apparently personal apothegm: 'I cannot cure myself of love / For what I thought you were before I knew you' (*SC* 5). In 'Two Cures for Love', one cure is getting 'to know him better' (*SC* 68).
12. Poison, *Every Rose Has its Thorn* (Capitol, 1988). This song reached number 1 in the US and number 13 in the UK during the poem's composition.
13. Atar Hadari, 'Cope, Pope and Philip Larkin', *About Larkin*, 7 (April 1999), 7–9, at 9.
14. Raine wrote to Cope admiringly on receiving the typescript in October 1989, and signed his letter 'Clint', in recognition. Wendy Cope archive, British Library, at MS89108/1/14.
15. This book contains forty-two illustrations by Nicholas Garland. The illustration of Clinton Thunder, with short-cropped beard, curly hair, and glasses, sporting an open-necked shirt, looks strikingly like Raine in several contemporaneous author photographs.

CHAPTER 7: 'THEY WAITED PATIENTLY': UNCOLLECTED COPE

1. *Desert Island Discs* (1 February 2019).
2. *Across the City* (London: Priapus, 1980), *Hope and the 42* (Leamington Spa: Other Branch Readings, 1984), *Poem from a Colour Chart of House Paints* (London: Priapus, 1986), *Does She Like Word-Games?* (London: Anvil, 1988), and *Men and Their Boring Arguments* (London: Wykeham, 1988).
3. Conversation with author, 8 August 2019.
4. Wendy Cope archive, British Library, at MS89108/1/90.
5. Wendy Cope archive, British Library, at MS89108/1/90.
6. Cope's private archive, Ely.
7. Marina Tsvetaeva, 'Poem of the Mountain', *Selected Poems*, trans. Elaine Feinstein (London: Penguin, 1971), 59.
8. Wendy Cope archive, British Library, at MS89108/1/91.
9. Wendy Cope archive, British Library, at MS89108/1/91.
10. John Cotton, 'The Priapus Press', *PN Review*, 21 (1981), 8.
11. Other poets included in the book were Duncan Forbes, Michael Hofmann, Medbh McGuckian, Blake Morrison, Simon Rae, and Joe Sheerin.
12. Later included in Wendy Cope, *Christmas Poems* (London: Faber, 2017), 23.
13. Many of her earlier, unpublished poems played with this conceit. In 1973, she drafted several short poems about trees with 'black

hands' or hands 'held still in helpless anger', and in 'Tradescantia' (1977), that plant is 'A headless body / All shoulders and fingers', desperate to 'escape // The death which creeps outwards from the roots'. Wendy Cope archive, British Library, at MS89108/1/90 and MS89108/1/91.

14. Don Paterson, *Rain* (London: Faber, 2009), 3.
15. Email correspondence with author (26 August 2019).
16. Wendy Cope, *Making Cocoa for Kingsley Amis* (promotional pamphlet) (London: Faber, 1985), 8.
17. *Hope and the 42*. No page numbers.
18. Wendy Cope archive, British Library, at MS89108/1/88.
19. Wendy Cope archive, British Library, at MS89108/1/88.
20. Wendy Cope archive, British Library, at MS89108/1/88.
21. William Shakespeare, *Shakespeare's Sonnets*, ed. Katherine Duncan-Jones (London: Arden, 2010), 169.
22. Wendy Cope archive, British Library, at MS89108/1/88.
23. Wendy Cope archive, British Library, at MS89108/1/88.
24. Wendy Cope archive, British Library, at MS89108/1/17.
25. Wendy Cope archive, British Library, at MS89108/1/89.
26. Email correspondence with author (26 August 2019).
27. *Does She Like Word-Games?* was published in a limited edition of 600 copies, and contains ten poems, six of which would later be included in *Serious Concerns*.
28. Email correspondence with author (15 June 2019). Cope goes on to say: 'Since I settled down, I may have done a bit of lifestyle boasting myself [...] but I haven't entirely abandoned the belief that poems are earned through suffering.'
29. Lilian Mohin, ed., *One Foot on the Mountain: An Anthology of British Feminist Poetry 1969–1979* (London: Onlywomen Press, 1979), 28. This book was popular enough to reach a third printing by 1982.
30. Wendy Cope, 'Introduction', *Is That the New Moon? Poems by Women Poets*, ed. Wendy Cope (1989) (2nd edn) (London: Collins, 2002), 9–12, at 10.
31. Wendy Cope, 'Feminism and Fiddles', *The Spectator* (1987) (*LLA* 260–2, at 261).
32. Wendy Cope archive, British Library, at MS89108/1/89.
33. Email correspondence with author (15 June 2019).
34. Wendy Cope and Boyana Petrovich, 'Very Fond of Bananas: Interview for Kingston University Website' (2013) (*LLA* 139–43, at 142).
35. This short pamphlet has no page numbers.
36. *The London Book of English Verse*, ed. Herbert Read and Bonamy Dobrée (London: Methuen, 1977), 196.

37. Stephen Regan, *The Sonnet* (Oxford: Oxford University Press, 2019), 374.
38. In 'A Cooking Egg'. T. S. Eliot, *Collected Poems 1909–1935* (New York: Harcourt, Brace and Company, 1930), 52. Wendy Cope archive, British Library, at MS89108/1/96. Regan claims that 'although' this rhyme has been borrowed, 'it retains its novelty and surprise' (374). Rather, it is demonstrably precisely the sort of theft Strugnell would have made.
39. A. A. Milne, *When We Were Very Young* (1924) (London: Methuen, 2004), 99.
40. *Acumen*, 26 (1996), 49.
41. Wendy Cope, *Wendy Cope Reading from Her Poems* (Poetry Archive, 2005), track 1.
42. Wendy Cope archive, British Library, at MS89108/1/54.
43. The poems are 'Ich glaub nicht an dem Himmel', 'Ich hab im Traum geweinet', and 'Herz, mein Herz, sei nicht beklommen'. In Cope's private archive, Ely.
44. Cope's archive reveals a comical and clever 'emergent poem' counterpart to 'The Lyric Poet', in which Heine's line 'Ich Weiss nicht, was soll es bedeuten' ('I don't know what it means') is mined for two nonsensical limericks. Wendy Cope archive, British Library, at MS89108/1/114.
45. Email correspondence with author (26 June 2019).
46. Heinrich Heine, *Selected Verse,* trans. Peter Boscombe (London: Penguin, 1968), 39.
47. Cope's private archive, Ely.
48. Wendy Cope archive, British Library, at MS89108/1/89.
49. Reprinted in Ewa Panecka, *Literature and the Monarchy: The Traditional and the Modern Concept of the Office of Poet Laureate of England* (Newcastle upon Tyne: Cambridge Scholars, 2014), 194, which also contains a discussion of the poem and its reception.
50. Andrew Motion, *Philip Larkin: A Writer's Life* (London: Faber, 1993), 510–11.
51. The poem was omitted from the final typescript. Wendy Cope archive, British Library, at MS89108/1/90 and MS89108/1/122.
52. *Metamorphosis: Poems Inspired by Titian* (London: National Gallery, 2012), ebook.
53. Wendy Cope, *Saint Hilda of Whitby* (Ely: Jericho Press, 2018). No page numbers; poem text on five pages. This is a handsome large-scale volume, printed on uncoated bond paper, and Cope's first small-press publication since the 1980s. 'I asked a neighbour with a printing press in his shed, J. F. Coakley of Jericho Press, if he was interested in doing a limited edition. I like what he's done.' Letter from Cope to author (26 February 2019).

54. Letter from Cope to author (26 February 2019).
55. Lay brothers were illiterate members of the monastic community, who performed manual work rather than worshiping God through book learning.
56. Bede, *Bede's Ecclesiastical History of England,* trans. A. M. Sellar (London: George Bell, 1907), 326.
57. According to Bede, her father, Hereric, a nephew of Edwin, King of Deira (which became part of the Kingdom of Northumbria in 654), was poisoned when Hilda was a small child, and she was then brought up in Edwin's court, converting to Christianity alongside him in her childhood (Bede, 325).
58. Bede, *Historia Ecclesiastica Gentis Anglorum,* iv <thelatinlibrary.com/bede/bede4.shtml#22> [accessed 23 August 2019].
59. Both versions are taken from Elaine Treharne, *Old and Middle English: An Anthology* (Oxford: Blackwell, 2000), 1–2.
60. In Bede's account, 'They expounded to him a passage of sacred history or doctrine, enjoining upon him, if he could, to put it into verse.' He returned the next morning with 'most excellent verse' and was then instructed 'to quit the secular habit, and take upon him monastic vows' (Bede, 333–4).
61. Bede writes that it was 'a quiet death' (Bede, 334).
62. Bede also mentions an unnamed nun at Whitby who 'saw [Hilda's] soul ascend to heaven in the company of angels; and this she openly declared, in the very same hour that it happened, to those handmaids of Christ that were with her; and aroused them to pray for her soul, even before the rest of the community had heard of her death'. This more closely echoes Cope's narrative, which conflates the two nuns (Bede, 334).
63. Email correspondence with author (20 June 2019).
64. 'Lord Heywood of Whitehall Obituary', *The Times* (5 November 2018) <thetimes.co.uk/article/lord-jeremy-heywood-of-whitehall-obituary-v5zpgq6f6> [accessed 23 April 2019].
65. Cope's private archive, Ely.
66. Cope's private archive, Ely.
67. Peter Walker, 'Boris Johnson calls David Cameron "Girly Swot" in Leaked Note', *The Guardian* (6 September 2019) <theguardian.com/politics/2019/sep/06/boris-johnson-calls-david-cameron-girly-swot-in-leaked-note> [accessed 30 September 2019].
68. Cope's private archive, Ely.
69. Email correspondence with author (29 December 2019).

Select Bibliography

Works by Wendy Cope

Cope is widely anthologised. Authored works and longer selections are listed below.

Across the City (London: Priapus, 1980). Pamphlet.
Anecdotal Evidence (London: Faber, 2018). Collection.
Being Boring (West Chester, PA, USA: Aralia, 1998). Pamphlet.
Christmas Poems (London: Faber, 2017). Collects twelve Christmas-themed poems, including three previously unpublished.
Does She Like Word-Games? (London: Anvil Press, 1988). Pamphlet.
Family Values (London: Faber, 2011). Collection.
Going for a Drive (London: Collins, 2010). Collection for children.
Hope and the 42 (Leamington Spa: Other Branch Readings, 1984). Pamphlet.
If I Don't Know (London: Faber, 2001). Collection.
Life, Love and The Archers (London: Two Roads, 2014). Selected prose.
Making Cocoa for Kingsley Amis (London: Faber, 1985). Promotional pamphlet.
Making Cocoa for Kingsley Amis (London: Faber, 1986). Collection.
Men and Their Boring Arguments (London: Wykeham, 1988). Pamphlet.
Ode to an Academic Problem (And the Solution) (Andover: International Thompson Publishing Services, 1990). Commissioned poem pamphlet.
Poem from a Colour Chart of House Paints (London: Priapus, 1986). Pamphlet.
Poetry Introduction 5 (London: Faber, 1982). Selection of early poems in anthology.
The River Girl (London: Faber, 1991). Book-length poem.
Saint Hilda of Whitby (Ely: Jericho Press, 2018). Pamphlet.
Serious Concerns (London: Faber, 1992). Collection.
Time for School (London: Collins, 2013). Poem for children.

Twiddling Your Thumbs: Hand Rhymes (London: Faber, 1988). Collection for children.

Two Cures for Love: Selected Poems 1979–2006 (London: Faber, 2008). Poems mainly selected from Cope's first three collections.

Wendy Cope Reading from Her Poems (Poetry Archive, 2005). Compact disc.

Works Edited by Wendy Cope

George Herbert, *George Herbert: Verse and Prose* (London: SPCK, 2002).

The Faber Book of Bedtime Stories (London: Faber, 2000).

The Funny Side: 101 Humorous Poems (London: Faber, 1998).

Heaven on Earth: 101 Happy Poems (London: Faber, 2001).

Is That the New Moon? (1989) (2nd edn) (London: Collins, 2002).

The Orchard Book of Funny Poems (London: Orchard, 1993).

Archive

Wendy Cope archive, British Library, London. Substantial archive of work and correspondence, up to 2011.

Wendy Cope private archive, Ely. Cope retains, at present, all post-2011 archive materials (including drafts and correspondence) at her private address, together with some earlier materials, mostly duplicates.

Criticism

Most criticism of Cope is confined to short reviews. Below is a select list of more substantial criticism.

Bennett, Andrew, 'Romantic Poets and Contemporary Poetry', *The Cambridge Companion to British Romantic Poetry*, ed. James Chandler and Maureen N. McLane (Cambridge: Cambridge University Press, 2008), 263–78. Includes assessment of Cope's use of Wordsworth.

Cambridge, Gerry, 'Poetic Assessment: Wendy Cope', *Acumen*, 26 (1996), 46–9. Short critical assessment of first two collections.

Hadari, Atar, 'Cope, Pope and Philip Larkin', *About Larkin*, 7 (April 1999), 7–9. Critical comparison of Cope to Larkin and Pope.

Juster, A. M., '"Anecdotal Evidence" in the Case of Wendy Cope', *Los Angeles Review of Books* (27 February 2018) < lareviewofbooks.org/article/anecdotal-evidence-in-the-case-of-wendy-cope/> [accessed 1 April 2019]. Review-essay.

Kane, Julie, 'Mortality and Mellowing: On Wendy Cope', *The Dark Horse*, 27 (2011), 90–5. Review-essay.

Novales, Marta Pérez, 'Wendy Cope's Use of Parody in *Making Cocoa for Kingsley Amis*', *Miscelánea: A Journal of English and American Studies*, 15 (1994), 481–500. Critical essay.

Rácz, István D., 'Heaneys of the Mind', *Hungarian Journal of English and American Studies*, 10.1/2 (2004), 127–36. Critical essay; includes focus on Cope's parodies.

Schmidt, Michael, *Lives of the Poets* (London: Phoenix, 1998). Wide-ranging critical book. Includes assessment of Cope.

Steele, Timothy, 'Verse Satire in the Twentieth Century', *A Companion to Satire*, ed. Ruben Quintero (Malden, MA, USA: Blackwell, 2007), 434–59. Includes contextualisation of Cope's satires.

Thompson, Nicola, 'Wendy Cope's Struggle with Strugnell in *Making Cocoa for Kingsley Amis*', *New Perspectives on Women and Comedy*, ed. Regina Barreca (Philadelphia, PA, USA: Gordon and Breach, 1992), 111–22. Critical essay.

Thwaite, Anthony, *Poetry Today: A Critical Guide to British Poetry 1960–95* (London: Routledge, 1996). Includes chapter on Tony Harrison, Douglas Dunn, James Fenton, and Wendy Cope.

Tondeur, Louise, 'Risk, Constraint, Play: A New Paradigm for Examining Practice-research in the Academy', *Text Journal*, 21.1 (2017) <textjournal.com.au/april17/tondeur.htm> [accessed 4 June 2019]. Includes analysis of Cope's 'A Policeman's Lot'.

Index

Printed and bound by CPI Group (UK) Ltd, Croydon, CR0 4YY

20/06/2023

03228591-0001